FOREWORD

S EVERAL months before the death of Dr. J. R. Miller, he made plans for " The Home Beautiful." The suggestion had been made to him that it would be helpful if he would take the heart of the books " Week Day Religion," " Practical Religion," " Home Making," and " In His Steps," and make a new volume on Christian home life. It was his purpose to improve on the suggestion made to him by preparing a number of new chapters. The plan was not to be carried out. God called him from earth before he was able to do more than begin the preparation of the volume.

However, he talked so fully of his plans to his associates, that it has been possible to arrange " The Home Beautiful " in a manner that is felt to be in accordance with the wishes of one whose life was devoted to inspiring men, women and children to the life that alone can make the home really beautiful.

JOHN T. FARIS

PHILADELPHIA, October, 1912

CONTENTS

THE HOME BEAUTIFUL

The Home Beautiful

I

THE WEDDED LIFE

HOMES are the divinely ordained fountains of life. It is not by accident that men live in families rather than solitarily. The human race began in a family, and Eden was a home. The divine blessing has ever rested upon nations and communities just in the measure in which they have adhered to these original institutions and have kept marriage and the home pure and holy; and blight and curse have come just in the measure in which they have departed from these divine models, dishonoring marriage and tearing down the sacred walls of home.

Back of the home lies marriage. The wedding day throws its shadow far down the future; it may be, ought to be, a shadow of healing and benediction.

In a tale of medieval English life a maiden goes before the bridal party on their way to the church, strewing flowers in their path. This was meant to signify that their wedded life should be one of joy and prosperity. Almost universally wedding ceremonies and festivities have some feature of similar significance, implying that the occasion is one of gladness. In some countries flowers are worn as bridal wreaths. In some they are woven into garlands for the waist, the tying of the ends being a part of the ritual. In others they are carried in the hand or worn in the hair or on the bosom. Music comes in, also, always joyous music, implying that the ceremony is one of peculiar gladness. In some places, too, wedding bells are rung, their peals being merry and gladsome.

All these and similar bridal customs indicate that the world regards the wedding as the crowning day of life, and marriage as an event of the highest felicity, an occasion for the most enthusiastic congratulations. Yet not always are these happy prophecies fulfilled. Sometimes the flowers wither and the music grows discordant and the wedding peals die away into a memory only of gladness. It ought not to be so. It is not so when the marriage has been true, and when the wedded life is ruled by love. Then the bridal wreath remains fresh and fragrant till it is laid upon the coffin by the loving hands of the one who survives to close the eyes of the other; and the wedding music and the peals of the bells continue to echo in tones of gladness and peace until hushed in sobbings of sorrow when the singers sing in dirges and the bells toll out the number of the finished years.

Marriage is intended to bring joy. The married life is meant to be the happiest, fullest, purest, richest life. It is God's own ideal of completeness. It was when he saw that it was not good for man to be alone that woman was made and brought to him to supply what was lacking. The divine intention, therefore, is that marriage shall yield happiness, and that it shall add to the fulness of the life of both husband and wife; that neither shall lose, but that both shall gain. If in any case it fails to be a blessing and to yield joy, and a richer, fuller life, the fault cannot be with the institution itself, but with those who under its shadow fail to fulfill its conditions.

The causes of failure may lie back of the marriage altar, for many are united in matrimony who never should have entered upon such a union; or they may lie in the life after marriage, for many who might attain to the very highest happiness in wedded life, fail to do so because they have not learned the secret of living happily together.

To guard against the former mistake the sacred character and the solemn responsibilities of marriage should be well understood and thoughtfully considered by all who would enter upon it. Marriage is a divine ordinance. It was part of God's original intention when he made man. It is not a mere human arrangement, something that sprang up in the race as a convenience along the history of the ages. It was not devised by any earthly lawgiver. It is not a habit into which men fell in the early days. The stamp of divine intention and ordination is upon it.

As a relationship it is the closest and most sacred on earth. The relation of parent and child is very close. Children are taught in all the Scriptures to honor their parents, to revere them, to cleave to them, to brighten and bless their lives in every possible way. Yet the marriage relation is put above the filial, for a man is to leave his father and his mother, give up his old home with all its sacred ties and memories, and cleave to his wife. After marriage a husband's first and highest duties are to his wife, and a wife's to her husband. The two are to live for each other. Life is to be lost for life. Every other interest is thenceforward secondary to the home interest.

Then the marriage relation is indissoluble. The two become in the fullest, truest sense one. Each is incomplete before; marriage is the uniting of two halves in one complete whole. It is the knitting together of two lives in a union so close and real that they are no more twain, but one; so close that nothing save death or the one crime of infidelity to the marriage bond itself can disunite them. Marriage, therefore, is not a contract which can be annulled at the will of one or both of the parties. It may be discovered after the marriage has been formed that the parties are ill mated; one may find in the other traits or habits unsuspected before, which seem to render happiness in union impossible; the husband may be cruel and abusive or the wife ill-tempered, thriftless or a burden; yet the Scriptures are very explicit in their teachings, that the tie once formed is indissoluble. There is one crime, said the pure and holy Jesus, which, committed by either, leaves the guilty one as dead, the other free. But besides this the teaching of Christ recognizes no other lawful sundering of the marriage tie. When two persons stand at the marriage altar and with clasped hands promise before God and in the presence of human witnesses to take each other as wife and as husband, to keep and to cherish each the other, only death can unclasp their hands. Each takes into sacred keeping the happiness and the highest good of the other to the end of life.

In view of the sacredness and indissolubleness of this relation, and the many tender and far-reaching interests that inhere in it, it is but the simplest commonplace to say that the greatest care should be taken before marriage to make sure that the union will be a true one, that the two lives will sweetly blend together, and that each will be able to make the other at least measurably happy. Yet obvious as is the fact, none the less is it profoundly important that it should be heeded. If there were more wise and honest forethought with regard to marriage, there would be less afterthought of regret and repenting.

Marriage is not the panacea for all life's ills. It does not of itself lead invariably and necessarily to all that is noble and beautiful in life. While its possibilities of happiness and blessing are so great, its possibilities of failure must not be ignored. Only a true and wise, only the truest and wisest, wedded life will realize the blessings of the ideal marriage relation.

The first lesson to be learned and practiced is loving patience. It requires some time to bring any two lives into perfect unison, so that they shall blend in every chord and tone. No matter how intimate the relations may have been before, neither knows much of the real life of the other until they meet with every separating wall and every thinnest veil removed.

In China the bridegroom does not see his bride until she is brought to him on his wedding day closely veiled and locked up in a sedan chair. The key is handed to him when the chair reaches his house, and he unlocks the door, lifts the veil and takes his first look at his treasure. Brides and bridegrooms with us are not usually such strangers to each other as among the "Celestials"; they see each other's face often enough, but it is doubtful whether as a rule they really know much more of each other's inner life. Even without any intention to hide their true selves or to appear veiled, it is only after marriage that their acquaintanceship becomes complete. There are graces of character and disposition that are then discovered for the first time; and there are also faults, peculiarities of habit, of taste, of temper, never suspected before, which then disclose themselves.

It is just at this point that one of the greatest

perils of wedded life is met. Some are disappointed
and discouraged by the discovery of these points
of uncongeniality, these possibilities of discord, con-
cluding at once that their marriage was a mistake
and must necessarily be a failure. Their beautiful
dream is shattered and they make no effort to build
it again. But really all that is needed is wise and
loving patience. There is no reason for discourage-
ment, much less for despair. It is entirely possible,
notwithstanding the discovery of these points of
friction and uncongeniality, to realize the highest
ideal of wedded life. It is like the meeting of two
rivers. At first there is confusion, excitement,
commotion, and apparent conflict and strife as the
two flow together, and it seems as if they never would
blend and commingle; but in a little time they unite
in one broad peaceful stream, rolling in majesty
and strength, without a trace of strife. So when
two independent lives, with diverse habits, tastes
and peculiarities first meet to be united in one, there
is embarrassment, there is perplexity, there is seem-
ing conflict, there is the dashing of life against life at
many points. Sometimes it may seem as if they
never could blend in one and as if the conflict
must go on hopelessly forever; but with loving
patience the two will in due time coalesce and unite
in one life, nobler, stronger, fuller, deeper, richer,
and move on in calmness and peace.

Perfect harmony cannot be forced in a day, can-
not indeed be forced at all, but must come through

gentleness and perhaps only after many days. There must be mutual adaptation, and time must be allowed for this. The present duty is unselfish love. Each must forget self in devotion to the other. Each must blame self and not the other when anything goes wrong. There must be the largest and gentlest forbearance. Impatience may wreck all. A sharp word may retard for months the process of soul-blending. There must be the determination on the part of both to make the marriage happy and to conquer everything that lies in the way. Then the very differences between the two lives will become their closest points of union. When they have passed through the process of blending, though it may for the time be painful and perilous, the result will be a wedded life of deep peace, quiet joy and inseparable affection.

Another secret of happiness in married life is courtesy. By what law of nature or of life is it that after the peals of the wedding bells have died away, and they have established themselves in their own home, so many husbands and wives drop the charming little amenities and refinements of manner toward each other that so invariably and delightfully characterized their intercourse before marriage? Is there no necessity for these civilities any longer? Are they so sure now of each other's love that they do not need to give expression to it, either in affectionate word or act? Is wedded love such a strong, vigorous and self-sufficing plant that it never needs sunshine, rain or dew? Is politeness merely a manner that is necessary in intercourse with the outside world, and not required when we are alone with those we love the best? Are home hearts so peculiarly constituted that they are not pained or offended by things that would never be pardoned in us if done in ordinary society? Are we under no obligations to be respectful and to pay homage to our dearest friends, while even to the rudest clown or the veriest stranger we meet outside our own doors we feel ourselves bound to show the most perfect civility?

On the contrary, there is no place in the world where the amenities of courtesy should be so carefully maintained as in the home. There are no hearts that hunger so for expressions of affection as the hearts of which we are most sure. There is no love that so needs its daily bread as the love that is strongest and holiest. There is no place where rudeness or incivility is so unpardonable as inside our own doors and toward our best beloved. The tenderer the love and the truer, the more it craves the thousand little attentions and kindnesses which so satisfy the heart. It is not costly presents at Christmas and on birthdays and anniversaries that are wanted; these are only mockeries if the days between are empty of affectionate expressions. Jewelry and silks and richly bound volumes will never atone for the want of warmth and tenderness. Between husband and wife there should be maintained, without break or pause, the most perfect courtesy, the gentlest attention, the most unselfish amiability, the utmost affectionateness. Coleridge says, "The happiness of life is made up of minute fractions, the little soon-forgotten charities of a kiss or a smile, a kind look, a heartfelt compliment, and the countless infinitesimals of pleasurable thought and genial feeling." These may seem trifles, and the omission of them may be deemed unworthy of thought; but they are the daily bread of love, and hearts go hungry when they are omitted. It may be only carelessness at first in a busy husband or a weary wife that fails in these small, sweet courtesies, and it may seem a little matter, but in the end the result may be a growing far apart of two lives which might have been forever very happy in each other had their early love but been cherished and nourished.

> "For love will starve if it is not fed,
> And true hearts pray for their daily bread."

Another important element in married life is unity of interest. There is danger that wedded lives drift apart because their employments are nearly always different. The husband is absorbed in business, in his profession, in severe daily toil; the wife has her home duties, her social life, her friends and friendships, her children; and the two touch at no point. Unless care is taken this separation of duties and engagements will lead to actual separation in heart and life. To prevent this each should keep up a constant, loving interest in whatever the other does. The husband may listen every evening to the story of the home life of the day, its incidents, its pleasures, its perplexities, its trials, the children's sayings and doings, what the neighbors said who dropped in, the bits of news that have been heard, and may enter with zest and sympathy into everything that is told him. Nothing that concerns the wife of his heart should be too small for even the gigantic intellect of the greatest of husbands. In personal biography few things are more charming and fascinating than the glimpses into the homes of some of the greatest men of earth, when we see them, having laid aside the cares and honors of the world, enter their own doors to romp with the children, to listen to their prattle, and to talk over with loving interest all the events and incidents of the day's home-history.

In like manner, every wise and true-hearted wife will desire to keep up an interest in all her husband's affairs. She will want to know of every burden, every struggle, every plan, every new ambition. She will wish to learn what undertaking has succeeded and what has failed, and to keep herself thoroughly familiar and in full sympathy with all his daily, personal life.

No marriage is complete which does not unite and blend the wedded lives at every point. This can be secured only by making every interest common to both. Let both hearts throb with the same joy and share each pang of sorrow. Let the same burdens rest on the shoulders of both. Let the whole life be made common.

In another sense still should their lives blend. They should read and study together, having the same line of thought, helping each other toward a higher mental culture. They should worship together, praying side by side, communing on the holiest themes of life and hope, and together carrying to God's feet the burdens of their hearts for their children and for every precious object. Why should they not talk together of their personal trials, their peculiar temptations, their infirmities, and help each other by sympathy, by brave word and by intercession, to be victorious in living?

Thus they should live one life as it were, not two. Every plan and hope of each should embrace the other. The moment a man begins to leave his wife out of any part of his life, or that she has plans, hopes, pleasures, friendships or experiences from which she excludes him, there is peril in the home. They should have no secrets which they keep from each other. They should have no companions or friends save those which they have in common. Thus their two lives should blend in one life, with no thought, no desire, no feeling, no joy or sorrow, no pleasure or pain, unshared.

Into the inner sanctuary of this wedded life no third party should ever be admitted. In its derivation the word home contains the idea of seclusion.

It shuts its inmates away from all the other life of the world about them. I have read of a young wife who prepared one little room in her house into which none but herself and her husband were ever to enter. The incident is suggestive. Even in the sanctuary of the home life there should be an inner Holy of holies, open only to husband and wife, into which no other eye ever shall peer, in which no other voice ever shall be heard to speak. No stranger should ever intermeddle with this holy life, no confidential friend should ever hear confidences from this inner sanctuary. No window or door should ever be opened into it, and no report should ever be carried out of what goes on within. The blended life they twain are living should be between themselves and God only.

Another rule for wedded life is to watch against every smallest beginning of misunderstanding or alienation. In the wreck of many a home there lingers still the memory of months or years of very tender wedded life. The fatal estrangement that rent the home asunder and made scandal for the world began in a little difference which a wise, patient word might have composed. But the word was not spoken — an unwise, impatient word was spoken instead — and the trivial breach remained unclosed, and grew wider till two hearts that had been knit together as one were torn forever apart. Rarely are estrangements the work of one day, or caused by one offense; they are growths.

"It is the little rift within the lute
 That by and by will make the music mute,
 And, ever-widening, slowly silence all —
 The little rift within the lover's lute:
 Or little pitted speck in garnered fruit,
 That, rotting inward, slowly molders all."

It is against the beginnings of alienations, therefore, that sacred watch must be kept. Has a hasty word been spoken? Instantly recall it and ask for forgiveness. Is there a misunderstanding? No matter whose the fault may be, do not allow it to remain one hour. Is the home life losing a little of its warmth? Ask not for the cause nor where the blame lies, but hasten to get back the old fervor at any cost. Never allow a second word to be spoken in a quarrel. Let not the sun go down upon an angry thought or feeling between two hearts that have been united as one. Pride must have no place in wedded life. There must never be any standing upon dignity, nor any nice calculation as to whose place it is to make the apology or to yield first to the other. True love knows no such casuistry; it seeks not its own; it delights in being foremost in forgiving and yielding. There is no lesson that husbands and wives need more to learn than instantly and always to seek forgiveness of each other whenever they are conscious of having in any way caused pain or committed a wrong. The pride that will never say, "I did wrong; forgive me," is not ready for wedded life.

To crown all, the presence of Christ should be sought at the marriage festivity and his blessing

on every day of wedded life. A lady was printing
on a blackboard a text for her little girl. The text
was: "Christ Jesus came into the world to save
sinners." Just as she had finished it the child
entered the room and began to spell out the words.
Presently she exclaimed, "Oh, mamma, you have
left out Jesus!" True enough, she had left out the
sacred name in transcribing the verse. It is a sad
omission when, in setting up their home, any husband
and wife leave out Jesus. No other omission they
could possibly make would cause so great a want in
the household. Without his presence to bless the
marriage, the congratulations and good wishes of
friends will be only empty words. Without his bene-
diction on the wedded life day by day, even the
fullest, richest tenderness of true affection will fail
to give all that is needed to satisfy hungry hearts.
Without the divine blessing, all the beauty, the
gladness, the treasure, which earth can give to a
home will not bring peace that may not any moment
be broken.

Surely too much is involved, too great responsi-
bility, too many and too precious interests, to ven-
ture upon wedded life without Christ. The lessons
are too hard to learn to be attempted without a
divine Teacher. The burdens are too heavy to be
borne without a mighty Helper. The perils of the
way are too many to be passed through without an
unerring Guide. The duties are too delicate, and
the consequences of failure in them too far-reaching

and too terrible, to be taken up without wisdom and help from above.

The prayer of the Breton mariner as he puts out on the waves is a fit prayer for every wedded life as its bark is launched: "Keep me, O God, for my boat is so small and the ocean is so wide."

II

THE HUSBAND'S PART

EACH member of the household has a part in the family life, and the fullest happiness and blessedness of the home can be attained only when each one's part is faithfully fulfilled. If any one member of the family fails in love or duty, the failure mars the whole household life, just as one discordant voice in a company of singers spoils the music, though all the others sing in perfect accord.

One person cannot alone make a home what it ought to be, what it might be. One sweet spirit may spread through the home the odors of love, even though among the other members there are bitterness and strife, just as one fragrant flower may spread through a hedge of thorns a breath of perfume. The influence of one gentle and unselfish life may also in time soften rudeness and melt selfishness, and pervade the home life with the blessedness of love. Yet still it is true that no one member of a household can make the household life full and complete. Each must do a part. The husband has a part, all his own, which no other one can do; the wife has a part; the children, the brothers, the sisters — each has his own part. Just as the different parts in music combine to produce harmony that pleases the ear, or as the artist's colors combine on his canvas to please the eye, or as the different parts of a machine work together to produce some effect of power, of motion, of delicacy, of skill; so when each member of the family is faithful in every duty and responsibility the result will be harmony, joy and blessedness.

What is the husband's part? How does the Word of God define his duties as a husband? What is involved on his part in the marriage relation? What does he owe to his wife? When he stands at the marriage altar and takes the hand of his bride in his and makes solemn vows and pledges in the presence of God and of human witnesses, what is it that he engages to do?

There is one word that covers all — the word love. "Husbands, love your wives," comes the command, with all divine authority, from the Holy Scriptures. The counsel is very short, but it grows exceedingly long when it is fully accepted and observed.

The art of the photographer is now so perfect that he can take the whole face of a great city newspaper on a plate small enough to be worn in a little pin; yet as you look at it under the microscope you find that every word is there, every point and mark. So in this word "love" we have a whole volume of thoughts and suggestions of life and duty crowded; and as we study it closely and carefully every one of them appears distinctly and clearly written out. What are some of the things that are embraced in a husband's love?

One is fondness, affectionate regard. When a man offers his hand in marriage to a woman he says by his act that his heart has made choice of her among all women, that he has for her a deeper and tenderer affection than for any other. At the marriage altar he solemnly pledges to her a continuance of that love until death. When the beauty has faded from her face and the luster from her eyes, when old age has brought wrinkles, or when sickness, care or sorrow has left marks of wasting or marring, the faithful husband's love is to remain deep and true as ever. His heart is still to choose his wife among all women and to find its truest delight in her.

But the word implies more than mere emotional fondness. The Scriptures give the measure of the love which husbands are to bear to their wives: "Husbands, love your wives, even as Christ also loved the Church and gave himself for it." There is no earthly line long enough to fathom the depths of Christ's love for his Church, and no mortal can love in the same degree; yet in so far as that love can be repeated on earth every husband is required to repeat it. Christ gave himself for his Church; the husband is to give himself, to deny himself, utterly to forget himself, in simple and whole-hearted devotion to his wife. In the true husband who realizes all that this divine command involves, selfishness dies at the marriage altar. He thinks no longer of his own comfort, but of his wife's. He takes the storm himself and shelters her from its blast. He toils to support her. He denies himself that he may bring new pleasures and comforts to her. He counts no sacrifice too great to be made which will bring benefit to her.

There is something very sacred and almost awe-inspiring in the act by which a wife, at her entrance into the marriage state, confides all the interests of her life to the hands of him whom she accepts as her husband. She leaves father and mother and the home of her childhood. She severs all the ties that bound her to her old life. She gives up the friends and the friendships of her youth. She cuts herself off from the sources of happiness to which she has been accustomed to turn. She looks up into the face of him who has asked her to be his wife, and with trembling heart yet with quiet confidence she entrusts to him and to his keeping all the sacred interests of her life. It is a holy trust which he receives when she thus commits herself to his hands. It is the lifelong happiness of a tender human heart capable of ineffable joy or unmeasured misery. It is the whole future well-being of a life which may be fashioned into the image of Christ, or marred and its beauty shattered forever.

The wife yields all up to the husband, gives herself in the fullest, completest sense. Will he be faithful to the holy trust reposed in his hands? Will he love her with an undecaying love? Will he shelter her from the blast and protect her in the day of peril? Will he cherish her happiness as a precious jewel, bearing all things, enduring all things, for her sake? Will he seek her highest good, help her to build up in herself the noblest womanhood? Is he worthy to receive into his keeping all that her confiding love lays at his feet? Will he be true to his trust forever?

It is a solemn thing for any man to assume such a trust and take a life, a gentle, delicate, confiding young life, into his keeping, to cherish, to shelter, to bless, until death either takes the trust out of his hands or strikes him down.

Every husband should understand that when a woman, the woman of his own free and deliberate choice, places her hand in his and thus becomes his wife, she has taken her life, with all its hopes and fears, all its possibilities of joy or sorrow, all its capacity for development, all its tender and sacred interests, and placed it in his hand, and that he is under the most solemn obligations to do all in his power to make that life happy, beautiful, noble and blessed. To do this he must be ready to make any personal sacrifice. Nothing less than this can be implied in loving as Christ loved his Church when he gave himself for it.

This love implies the utmost gentleness in manner. One may be very faithful and true and yet lack that affectionateness in speech and act which has such power to satisfy the heart. One of the special Scripture admonitions to husbands is that they love their wives and be not bitter against them. It is a counsel against all display of ill-temper, all bitter feelings as well as angry words and unkind acts. The teaching of the passage strictly interpreted is that all bitterness should be suppressed in the very workings of the heart and changed into sweetness.

Are all husbands blameless in this respect? Are there none who are sometimes bitter against their wives? Are there none who sometimes speak sharp words that strike and sting like arrows in their hearts? It must be in thoughtlessness, for no true man who really loves his wife would intentionally cause her pain. The poet Cowper suggested a very subtle test of character when he wrote —

> I would not enter on my list of friends,
> Though graced with manners and fine sense
> (Yet wanting sensibility), the man
> Who needlessly sets foot upon a worm.

Yet there are men who would not willingly tread upon a crawling insect or a worm, who would not injure a dumb animal nor needlessly hurt any of the lowest of God's creatures, who every day bring many a pang to the heart of the tender, faithful, loving wife of their bosom by their sharp words or their impatient looks or acts.

The trouble is that men fall into free and careless habits at home. They are not so in society; they are gentle to other women. They pride themselves on their thoughtfulness. They are careful not even by tone or look to hurt a sensitive spirit. But at home too often they are rude, careless in speech and heedless of the effect of their words and actions. They blurt out in their own houses the ill-humor they have suppressed all day on the street. They answer proper questions in an irritated tone. They speak impatiently on the slightest provocation. They are sullen, morose and unsocial. They forget that their own wives are women with gentle spirits, easily hurt. A man thinks that because a woman is his wife she should understand him, that she should know that he loves her even if he is rude to her, that she should not mind anything he says or does, even if it is something that would sorely hurt or offend any other woman.

There never was a falser premise than this. Just because she is his wife he owes her the loftiest courtesy that it is in his nature to pay. There is no other woman in all the world that feels so keenly the sting of sharp or thoughtless words from his lips as his own wife, and there is no other of whose feelings he should be so careful and whom he should so grieve to hurt. No other has the claim upon his thoughtfulness and affection that she has. Love gives no license for rudeness or incivility to the one who is loved. The closer the relationship, the more are hearts pained by any look, tone, gesture or word that tells of bitterness or even of thoughtlessness.

But it is not enough that men be not bitter against their wives. The mere absence of a fault or vice is not a virtue. Silence is no doubt better than bitterness. Even stateliness, though cold as a marble statue, is possibly better than rudeness. A garden without weeds, though having neither plant nor flower, is better than a patch of weeds; but a garden beautiful and fragrant with flowers is better still. It is a step in the right direction when a husband is not bitter against his wife, and it is a good deal farther in the right direction when, instead of being bitter, his words and acts and whole bearing are characterized by gentleness and affectionateness. There are men who speak no bitter words, no sharp, petulant words, and yet but few kindly, tender words fall from their lips. The old warmth of the lover and the newly wed husband has died out and the speech is businesslike and cold. No one needs to be told that there is nothing in such a bearing to satisfy a heart that craves the richest things true love can give.

Words seem little things, so fleeting and evanescent that apparently it cannot matter much of what sort they are. They are so easily spoken that we forget what power they have to give pleasure or pain. They seem so swiftly gone that we forget they do not go away at all, but linger either like barbed arrows in the heart where they struck, or like fragrant flowers distilling perfume. They seem so powerless for good or ill, and we do not remember that they either tear down or build up fair fabrics of joy and peace in the souls of those to whom we speak.

While gentleness should always mark a husband's bearing toward his wife, there are occasions which call for peculiar thoughtfulness and sympathetic expression. Sometimes she is very weary. The cares of the day have been unusually trying. Matters have not gone smoothly at home. Her quivering nerves have been sorely overtaxed. She has heard sad news. A child has been sick all day, or, worse still, has by some disobedience or some wrongdoing almost broken her heart. What is a husband's part at such times? Surely if he is capable of tenderness he will show it now. He will not utter a word to add to the load the overburdened spirit is already carrying. He will seek rather by every thoughtful help his love can give to lighten the burden, to quiet the trembling heart and to impart strength and peace.

In walking on the street one day in a violent and sudden storm, as I was passing under a tree a weary bird fluttered down from among the branches, and alighting on my bosom crept under my coat. It was seeking a refuge from the fierce storm. Every wife should know that she will always find in her husband's love a safe and quiet refuge when she is perplexed or tried. She should be sure that he will understand her, that he will deal most gently with her, that he will give his own strength to shelter her, that he will impart of his own life to build up the waste in hers. She should never have to doubt that he will sympathize with her in whatever it may be that tries her. She should never have to fear repulse or coldness or rebuke when she flees to him for shelter. What Christ is to his people in their weariness, their sorrow, their pain, their alarm, every husband in his own little measure should be to his own wife.

There is one place where we shall remember every unkindness and every neglect shown to those who lean upon us for support and for sympathy, and then the pain will be ours if we have failed in tenderness. Ruskin says: "He who has once stood beside the grave, to look back upon the companions on whom it has been forever closed, feeling how impotent there is the wild love or the keen sorrow to give one instant's pleasure to the pulseless heart, or atone in the lowest measure to the departed spirit for the hour of unkindness, will scarcely for the future incur that debt to the heart which can only be discharged to the dust." Yet how slow we all are to learn this lesson!

It is of little avail to bring flowers to a wife's coffin when you failed to strew flowers on the path while her weary feet were painfully walking over it. It is of little avail to speak her praises now in every ear, to recount her excellences and dwell upon her virtues, when in her lifetime you never had a word of praise for her own ears, nor a loving compliment, nor any token to show to her how much you prized her.

The time to show love's tenderness is when it is needed; if we have failed then, the duty never can be rendered at all. No after-atonement of lavish affection can brighten the hours that were left unbrightened in passing, or lighten the burdens that were left unlightened when the weary spirit was bowing under them.

The spirit of this love requires a husband to honor his wife. He honored her before she was his wife. He saw in her his ideal of all that was noble, lovely and queenly. He showed her every mark of honor of which his soul was capable. Now that he has lifted her up to the throne of his heart, will he honor her less? Not less, but more and ever more, if he be a true husband and a manly man. He has taken her now into the closest and holiest relation of earth. He has linked her life with his own, so that henceforward whatever affects one affects both. If one is honored the other is exalted; if one is dishonored the other is debased. There is infinitely more reason why he should honor her now than before she was his wife.

The ways in which he should show her honor are countless. He will do it by providing for her wants on as generous a scale as his position and his means will justify. He will do it by making her the sharer of all his own life. He will counsel with her about his business, advise with her concerning every new plan and confide to her at every point the results of his undertakings. A true wife is not a child. When he chose her to be his wife he believed her to be worthy.

"I can give you my answer tomorrow," a man said to one who had asked him to invest in a certain property, "I must speak to my wife about it first, as I have learned to value her advice." "Bah!" was the reply, "I never talk to my wife about business." Yet this man would have been saved from many mistakes if only he had taken his sensible wife into his counsels. Others who knew her, delight to consult her, for her words were well-considered and her judgment was always good.

But even if she is not qualified to give him great aid in his business plans, she loves him and is deeply interested in everything that he is doing. She is made happy by being taken into all his counsels, and thus lifted up close beside him in his life-work; and he is made stronger, too, for energetic duty and for heroic achievement by her warm sympathy and by the inspiration of her cheerful encouragement. Whether the day bring defeat or victory, failure or success, he should confide all to her in the evening. If the day has been prosperous she has a right to share the gratification; if it has been adverse, she will want, as a true wife, to help her husband bear his burden and to whisper a new word of courage in his heart. Not only then does a man fail to give his wife due honor when he shuts her out of his own business life, but he also robs himself of that inspiration and help which every true wife is able to minister to her husband.

It is not in an unkind or a selfish spirit that he

withholds from her these trying and painful things; indeed, ofttimes it is the very tenderness of his regard for his wife that leads him to keep from her things that would cause her distress or anxiety of mind. He does not suppose that she could help him in the solving of the perplexing questions or in the bearing of the heavy burdens, and he thinks it would be unkindness in him to vex her with the questions or oppress her with the burdens. So he keeps these troublous things to himself, and ofttimes while he is in deep anxiety and bowing under heavy loads, wellnigh crushed beneath them, she is moving along in a path of sunshine, in quiet enjoyment, with no shadow of care, wholly unconscious of her husband's need of strong sympathy and help. Though this was the prompting of affectionate unselfishness in the husband, there is no doubt that in ordinary circumstances such a course is both wrong and unwise. It is robbing the wife of love's privilege of sharing the whole of her husband's life. It is treating her as if she were a child unable to understand the husband's affairs or to help him carry his load. It is taking from her the deep and exquisite joy which every true wife finds in suffering with her husband in whatever causes him pain or loss.

When a man has taken a woman to be his wife, he has linked her life with his own in the closest of all earthly relations. Whatever concerns him also concerns her. He has no interests which are not hers as well as his. He should, therefore, make her the sharer of all his life. No remotest corner of it should be closed against her. She should know of his successes and triumphs and be permitted to rejoice with him in his gladness. If reverses come, she should know also of these, that she may sympathize with him, encourage and help him in his struggles and stand close beside him when the shadow rests upon him. They have linked their lives together "for better or worse," and they should share the pains and the trials as well as the pleasures and the comforts that come to either of them. A true wife is not a child; she is a woman, and should be treated as a woman.

A man does deep injustice to the woman he has chosen to be his wife when he thinks that she is too frail and delicate to endure with him the storms that blow upon him, or that she is too inexperienced or too ignorant of life to discuss with him the problems that cause him grave and earnest thought. She may not have all his practical wisdom with regard to the world's affairs, and yet she may be able to offer many a suggestion which shall prove of more value to him than the counsel of shrewd men of the world. Woman's quick intuition often sees at a glance what man's slow logic is long in discovering. There is many a man whose success would have been greater far, or to whom failure would not have come, had he but sought or accepted his wife's counsel and help. Even if a wife can give no real practical aid, her husband will be made ten times stronger in his own

heart by her strengthening sympathy and brave cheer
while he is carrying his load or fighting his battle.

It need scarcely even be said, further, that a husband should honor his wife by being worthy of her.
Love has been the inspiration that has lifted many
a man from a lowly place to lofty heights of worth
or power. Many a youth of humble origin and
without rank or condition has worshiped at the feet
of a maiden far above him in social standing, and,
incited by his ardent affection, has made himself
worthy of her and then won her as his bride.

Quintin Matsys, the celebrated painter, was in
his youth a blacksmith at Antwerp. He loved the
beautiful daughter of a painter and was loved in
return; but her father was inexorable. "Wert thou
a painter," he said, "she should be thine; but a
blacksmith — never!" The young man was not
discouraged. The hammer dropped from his hand.
A new life began to stir within him. A thousand
glorious conceptions began to flit like shadows across
his brain. "I will be a painter," he said. He
thought of his utter ignorance of art, without any
technical knowledge, and was cast down at first.
But he began, and his first efforts encouraged him.
He took the pencil, and the lines that came were
the features of the face that glowed in his heart.
Inspired by love he wrought on. "I will paint her
portrait," he said; and the colors flashed upon his
canvas till the likeness was perfect. He took it to
the father. "There," said he, "I claim the prize,

for I am a painter now." He won his bride by making himself worthy of her. Under the inspiration of love he continued to paint, winning new victories of genius, becoming eminent among artists, and, dying, was buried with high honors in the cathedral of his native city. The grand motive of his life was to become worthy of her whom he desired to win.

Every true-hearted husband should seek to be worthy of the wife he has already won. For her sake he should reach out after the noblest achievements and strive to attain the loftiest heights of character. To her he is the ideal of all that is manly, and he should seek to become every day more worthy of the homage she pays to him. Every possibility in his soul should be developed. Every latent power and energy of his life should be brought out. His hand should be trained under love's inspiration to do its most skillful work. Every fault in his character should be eradicated, every evil habit conquered, and every hidden beauty of soul should burst into fragrant bloom for her sake. She looks to him as her ideal of manhood, and he must see to it that the ideal is never marred — that he never falls by any unworthy act of his own from the high pedestal in her heart to which she has raised him. Among all sins few are worse than those by which a man draws down shame and reproach upon himself, for, besides all the sorrow he brings upon her in so many other ways, he thus crushes in his wife's heart the fair and noble image of manhood which she had enshrined there next to her Saviour's.

In the spirit of this love every husband should be a large-hearted man. He should never be a tyrant, playing the petty despot in his home. There is no surer mark than this of a small man. A manly man has a generous spirit which shows itself in all his life, but nowhere so richly as within his own doors. There are wives whose natures do not blossom out in their best beauty because the atmosphere in which they live is chill and cold. A lady who is always watching for beautiful things and gathering them about her brought from the mountain-side a sod of moss. She put it in her parlor, and after a while, in the genial warmth, there sprang out from the bosom of the moss a multitude of sweet, delicate spring flowers. The seeds had long lain in the moss but in the cold air of the mountain they had never burst into life. There are noble wives in homes humble and homes stately who are just like this moss. In their natures there are the germs of many excellences and the possibilities of rich outcome, but the home-atmosphere is repressing and chilly, and in it none of these richer qualities and powers manifest themselves. The bringing of new warmth into the home will draw out these latent germs of unsuspected loveliness. The husband who would have his wife's nature blossom out into its best possibilities of character, influence and power must make a genial summer atmosphere for his home all the year round.

Then this large-heartedness will impart its spirit to the home itself. A husband who is generous within his own doors will not be close and niggardly outside. The heart that is used always to be open at home cannot be carried shut through this suffering world. The prosperous home of a generous man sends many a blessing and comfort out to less-favored homes. Every true home ought to be a help to a great many struggling lives. Every generous and large-hearted man scatters many a comfort among the needy and the suffering as he passes through this world.

There is nothing lost by such scattering. No richer blessing can come upon a home than the benedictions of those who have been helped, who have been fed at its doors, or sheltered beneath its roof, or inspired by its cheer and kindly interest. There is no memorial that any man can make for himself in this world so lasting and so satisfying as that which a life of unselfish kindness and beneficence builds up.

One thing more may be said: Every husband of a Christian wife should walk with her in common love for Christ. There are some husbands, however, who fail in this. They love their wives very sincerely, and make many sacrifices for their sake. They carefully shelter them from life's rude blasts. They bless them with all tenderness and affectionateness. They honor them very highly, bringing many a noble achievement to lay at their feet, and showing them all homage and respect. They do everything that love can suggest to make their earthly happiness full and complete. They share every burden and walk close beside them in every way of trial. But when they come to the matter of personal religion they draw back and leave them to go alone. While the wife goes into the sanctuary to worship the husband waits without. At the very point where his interest in her life should be deepest it fails altogether.

Surely it is a great wrong to a woman, tender and dependent, to leave her to walk alone through this world in her deepest life, receiving no sympathy, no companionship, no support, from him who is her dearest friend. She must leave him outside of the most sacred part of her life. She must be silent to him concerning the experiences of her soul in its spiritual struggles, aspirations, yearnings, hopes. She must bear alone the responsibility of the children's religious nurture and training. Alone she must bow in prayer before God. Alone she must sit at the Lord's table.

It cannot be right that a husband should leave his wife to live such a large part of her life without his companionship and sympathy. His love should seek to enter with her into every sacred experience. In no other way could he give her such joy as by taking his place beside her as a fellow heir of the same grace. It would lighten every burden, since he would now share it with her. It would bring new radiance to her face, new peace to her heart,

new zest to all life for her. It would make their
marriage more perfect and unite their hearts in a
closer union, since only those realize the full sweet-
ness of wedded life who are one at every point and
in every feeling, purpose and hope, and whose souls
blend in their higher, spiritual part as well as in
their lower nature and experiences. Then it would
also introduce the husband himself to sources of
blessing and strength of which he has never known
before; for the religion of Christ is a reality and
brings the soul into communication with God and
with infinite springs of comfort, help and blessing.
In sharing her life of faith and prayer he would
find his own life linked to heaven.

United, then, on earth in a common faith in Christ,
their mutual love mingling and blending in the love
of God, they shall be united also in heaven in eternal
fellowship. Why should hearts spend years on earth
in growing into one, knitting life to life, blending soul
in soul, for a union that is not to reach beyond the
valley of shadows? Why not weave for eternity?

III

THE WIFE'S PART

IT is a high honor for a woman to be chosen from among all womankind to be the wife of a good and true man. She is lifted up to be a crowned queen. Her husband's manly love laid at her feet exalts her to the throne of his life. Great power is placed in her hands. Sacred destinies are reposed in her keeping. Will she wear her crown beneficently? Will she fill her realm with beauty and with blessing? Or will she fail in her holy trust? Only her married life can be the answer.

A woman may well pause before she gives her hand in marriage, and inquire whether he is worthy to whom she is asked to surrender so much; whether he can bring true happiness to her life; whether he can meet the cravings of her nature for love and for companionship; whether he is worthy to be lifted to the highest place in her heart and honored as a husband should be honored. She must ask these questions for her own sake, else the dream may fade with the bridal wreath, and she may learn, when too late, that he for whom she has left all and to whom she

[87]

has given all is not worthy of the sacred trust, and has no power to fill her life with happiness, to wake her heart's chords, to touch her soul's depths.

But the question should be turned and asked from the other side. Can she be a true wife to him who asks for her hand? Is she worthy of the love that is laid at her feet? Can she be a blessing to the life of him who would lift her to the throne of his heart? Will he find in her all the beauty, all the tender love-liness, all the rich qualities of nature, all the deep sympathy and companionship, all the strengthful, uplifting love, all the sources of joy and help, which he seems now to see in her? Is there any possible future for him which she could not share? Are there needs in his soul, or hungers, which she cannot answer? Are there chords in his life which her fingers cannot wake?

Surely it is proper for her to question her own soul for him while she bids him question his soul for her. A wife has a part in the song of wedded love if it is to be a harmony. She holds in her hands on her wedding day precious interests, sacred des-tinies and holy responsibilities, which, if disclosed to her sight at once, might well appall the bravest heart. Her opportunity is one which the loftiest angel might covet. Not the happiness only of a manly life, but its whole future of character, of influence, of growth, rests with her.

What is the true ideal of a wife? It is not some-thing lifted above the common experiences of life,

not an ethereal angel feeding on ambrosia and moving
in the realms of fancy. In some European cities
they sell to the tourist models of their cathedrals
made of alabaster, whiter than snow. But so deli-
cate are these alabaster shrines that they must be
kept under glass covers or they will be soiled by the
dust, and so frail that they must be sheltered from
every rude touch, lest their lovely columns may be
shattered. They are very graceful and beautiful,
but they serve no lofty purpose. No worshipers
can enter their doors. No melody rises to heaven
from their aisles. So there are ideals of womanhood
which are very lovely, full of graceful charms, pleas-
ing, attractive, but which are too delicate and frail
for this prosaic, storm-swept world of ours. Such
ideals the poets and the novelists sometimes give
us. They appear well to the eye as they are por-
trayed for us on the brilliant page. But of what
use would they be in the life which the real woman
of our day has to live? A breath of earthly air would
stain them. One day of actual experience in the hard
toils and sore struggles of life would shatter their
frail loveliness to fragments. We had better seek
for ideals which will not be soiled by a rude touch
nor blown away by a stiff breeze, and which will
grow lovelier as they move through life's paths of
sacrifice and toil. The true wife needs to be no mere
poet's dream, no artist's picture, no ethereal lady
too fine for use, but a woman healthful, strong,
practical, industrious, with a hand for life's common

duties, yet crowned with that beauty which a high and noble purpose gives to a soul.

One of the first essential elements in a wife is faithfulness, faithfulness, too, in the largest sense. "The heart of her husband doth safely trust in her." Perfect confidence is the basis of all true affection. A shadow of doubt destroys the peace of married life. A true wife by her character and by her conduct proves herself worthy of her husband's trust. He has confidence in her affection; he knows that her heart is unalterably true to him. He has confidence in her management; he confides to her the care of his household. He knows that she is true to all his interests — that she is prudent and wise, not wasteful nor extravagant. It is one of the essential things in a true wife that her husband shall be able to leave in her hands the management of all domestic affairs, and know that they are safe. Wifely thriftlessness and extravagance have destroyed the happiness of many a household and wrecked many a home. On the other hand, many a man owes his prosperity to his wife's prudence and her wise administration of household affairs.

Every true wife makes her husband's interests her own. While he lives for her, carrying her image in his heart and toiling for her all the days, she thinks only of what will do him good. When burdens press upon him she tries to lighten them by sympathy, by cheer, by the inspiration of love. She enters with zest and enthusiasm into all his plans.

THE WIFE'S PART

She is never a weight to drag him down; she is strength in his heart to help him ever to do nobler and better things.

All wives are not such blessings to their husbands. Woman is compared sometimes to the vine, while man is the strong oak to which it clings. But there are different kinds of vines. Some wreathe a robe of beauty and a crown of glory for the tree, covering it in summer days with green leaves and in the autumn hanging among its branches rich purple clusters of fruit; others twine their arms about it only to sap its very life and destroy its vigor, till it stands decaying and unsightly, stripped of its splendor, discrowned and fit only for the fire.

A true wife makes a man's life nobler, stronger, grander, by the omnipotence of her love "turning all the forces of manhood upward and heavenward." While she clings to him in holy confidence and loving dependence she brings out in him whatever is noblest and richest in his being. She inspires him with courage and earnestness. She beautifies his life. She softens whatever is rude and harsh in his habits or his spirit. She clothes him with the gentler graces of refined and cultured manhood. While she yields to him and never disregards his lightest wish, she is really his queen, ruling his whole life and leading him onward and upward in every proper path.

But there are wives also like the vines which cling only to blight. Their dependence is weak, indolent helplessness. They lean but impart no strength. They cling but they sap the life. They put forth no hand to help. They loll on sofas or promenade the streets; they dream over sentimental novels; they gossip in drawing rooms. They are utterly useless, and being useless they become burdens even to manliest, tenderest love. Instead of making a man's life stronger, happier, richer, they absorb his strength, impair his usefulness, hinder his success and cause him to be a failure among men. To themselves also the result is wretchedness. Dependence is beautiful when it does not become weakness and inefficiency. The true wife clings and leans, but she also helps and inspires. Her husband feels the mighty inspiration of her love in all his life. Toil is easier, burdens are lighter, battles are less fierce, because of the face that waits in the quiet of the home, because of the heart that beats in loving sympathy whatever the experience, because of the voice that speaks its words of cheer and encouragement when the day's work is done. No wife knows how much she can do to make her husband honored among men, and his life a power and a success, by her loyal faithfulness, by the active inspiration of her own sweet life.

The good wife is a good housekeeper. I know well how unromantic this remark will appear to those whose dreams of married life are woven of the fancies of youthful sentiment; but these frail dreams of sentiment will not last long amid the stern real-

ities of life, and then that which will prove one of
the rarest elements of happiness and blessing in the
household will be housewifely industry and diligence.

When young people marry they are rarely troubled
with many thoughts about the details of housekeep-
ing. Their dreams are high above all such common-
places. The mere mention of such things as cooking,
baking, sweeping, dusting, mending, ironing, jars
upon the poetic rhythm of the lofty themes of con-
versation. It never enters the brains of these happy
lovers that it can make any difference in the world
in their home life whether the bread is sweet or
sour, whether the oatmeal is well cooked or scorched,
whether the meals are punctual or tardy. The mere
thought that such sublunary matters could affect
the tone of their wedded life seems a desecration.

It is a pity to dash away such exquisite dreams,
but the truth is they do not long outlast the echo
of the wedding peals or the fragrance of the bridal
roses. The newly married are not long within
their own doors before they find that something
more than tender sentiment is needed to make their
home life a success. They come down from the
clouds when the daily routine begins and touch the
common soil on which the feet of other mortals walk.
Then they find that they are dependent, just like
ordinary people, on some quite prosaic conditions.
One of the very first things they discover is the inti-
mate relation between the kitchen and wedded happi-
ness. That love may fulfill its delightful prophecies

and realize its splendid dreams there must be in the new home a basis of material and very practical elements. The palace that is to rise into the air, shooting up its towers, displaying its wonders of architecture, flashing its splendors in the sunshine, the admiration of the world, must have its foundation in commonplace earth, resting on plain, hard, honest rock. Love may build its palace of noble sentiments and tender affections and sweet charities, rising into the very clouds, and in this splendid home two souls may dwell in the enjoyment of the highest possibilities of wedded life; but this palace, too, must stand on the ground, with unpoetic and unsentimental stones for its foundation. That foundation is good housekeeping. In other words, good breakfasts, dinners and suppers, a well-kept house, order, system, promptness, punctuality, good cheer — far more than any young lovers dream does happiness in married life depend upon such commonplace things as these. Love is very patient, very kind, very gentle; and where there is love no doubt the plainest fare is ambrosia and the homeliest surroundings are charming. I know the wise man said: "Better is a dinner of herbs where love is, than a stalled ox [*i.e.*, a good roast-beef dinner], with hatred therewith"; but herbs as a constant diet will pall on the taste, especially if poorly served, even if love is ever present to season them. In this day of advanced civilization it ought to be possible to have both the stalled ox and love. Husbands are not angels in this mundane state, and not being such they need a substantial basis of good housekeeping for the realization of their dreams of blissful home-making.

There certainly have been cases in which very tender love has lost its tenderness and when the cause lay in the disorder, the negligence and the mismanagement of the housewifery. There is no doubt that many a heart-estrangement begins at the table where meals are unpunctual and food is poorly cooked or repulsively served. Bad housekeeping will soon drive the last vestige of romance out of any home. The illusion which love weaves about an idolized bride will soon vanish if she proves incompetent in her domestic management. The wife who will keep the charm of early love unbroken through the years, and in whose home the dreams of the wedding day will come true, must be a good housekeeper.

In one of his Epistles St. Paul gives the counsel that young wives should be "workers at home," as the Revisers have put it, signifying that home is the sphere of the wife's duties, and that she is to find her chief work there. There is a glory in all the Christian charities which Christian women, especially in these recent days, are founding and conducting with so much enthusiasm and such marked and abounding success. Woman is endowed with gifts of sympathy, of gentleness, of inspiring strengthfulness, which peculiarly fit her to be Christ's messenger of mercy to human wo and sorrow and pain.

There is the widest opportunity in the most fitting service for every woman whose heart God has touched to be a ministering angel to those who need sympathy or help. There are many who are free to serve in public charities, in caring for the poor, for the sick in hospital wards, for the orphaned and the aged. There are few women who cannot do a little in some one or more of these organizations of Christian beneficence.

But it should be understood that for every wife the first duty is the making and keeping of her own home. Her first and best work should be done there, and till it is well done she has no right to go outside to take up other duties. She is to be a "worker at home." She must look upon her home as the one spot on earth for which she alone is responsible, and which she must cultivate well for God if she never does anything outside. For her the Father's business is not attending Dorcas societies, and missionary meetings, and mothers' meetings, and temperance conventions, or even teaching a Sunday-school class, until she has made her own home all that her wisest thought and best skill can make it. There have been wives who in their zeal for Christ's work outside have neglected Christ's work inside their own doors. They have had eyes and hearts for human need and human sorrow in the broad fields lying far out, but neither eye nor heart for the work of love close about their own feet. The result has been that while they were doing angelic work in the lanes and streets, the angels were mourning over their neglected duties within the hallowed walls of their own homes. While they were winning a place in the hearts of the poor or the sick or the orphan, they were losing their rightful place in the hearts of their own household. Let it be remembered that Christ's work in the home is the first that he gives to every wife, and that no amount of consecrated activities in other spheres will atone in this world or the next for neglect or failure there.

The good wife is generous and warm-hearted. She does not grow grasping and selfish. In her desire to economize and add to her stores she does not forget those about her who suffer or want. While she gives her wisest and most earnest thought and her best and most skillful work to her own home, her heart does not grow cold toward those outside who need sympathy. I cannot conceive of true womanhood ripened into mellow richness, yet wanting the qualities of gentleness and unselfishness. A woman whose heart is not touched by the sight of sorrow, and whose hands do not go out in relief where it is in her power to help, lacks one of the elements which make the glory of womanhood.

This is not the place to speak of woman as a ministering angel. If it were it would be easy to fill many pages with the bright records of most holy deeds of self-sacrifice. I am speaking now, however, of woman as wife; and only upon so much of this ministry to the suffering as she may perform in her own home, at her own door and in connection with her housewifely duties is it fit to linger at this time. But even in this limited sphere her opportunities are by no means small.

It is in her own home that this warmth of heart and this openness of hand are first to be shown. It is as wife and mother that her gentleness performs its most sacred ministry. Her hand wipes away the teardrops when there is sorrow. In sickness she is the tender nurse. She bears upon her own heart every burden that weighs upon her husband. No matter how the world goes with him during the day, when he enters his own door he meets the fragrant atmosphere of love. Other friends may forsake him, but she clings to him with unalterable fidelity. When gloom comes down and adversity falls upon him, her faithful eyes look ever into his like two stars of hope shining in the darkness. When his heart is crushed, beneath her smile it gathers itself again into strength, "like a wind-torn flower in the sunshine." "You cannot imagine," wrote De Tocqueville of his wife, "what she is in great trials. Usually so gentle, she then becomes strong and energetic. She watches me without my knowing it; she softens, calms and strengthens me in difficulties which distract me, but leave her serene." An eloquent tribute, but one which thousands of husbands might give. Men often see not the angel in the plain, plodding woman who walks quietly beside them, until the day of trial comes; then in

the darkness the glory shines out. An angel minis-
tered to our Lord when in Gethsemane he wrestled
with his great and bitter sorrow. What a benedic-
tion to the mighty Sufferer was in the soft gliding
to his side of that gentle presence, in the touch of
that soothing, supporting hand laid upon him, in
the comfort of that gentle voice thrilling with sym-
pathy as it spoke its strengthening message of love!
Was it a mere coincidence that just at that time and
in that place the radiant messenger came? No, it
is always so. Angels choose such occasions to pay
their visits to men.

> "With silence only as their benediction
> God's angels come,
> Where in the shadow of a great affliction
> The soul sits dumb."

So it is in the dark hours of a man's life, when bur-
dens press, when sorrows weigh like mountains upon
his soul, when adversities have left him crushed and
broken, or when he is in the midst of fierce struggles
which try the strength of every fiber of his man-
hood, that all the radiance and glory of a true wife's
strengthful love shine out before his eyes. Only
then does he recognize in her God's angel of mercy.

> "O woman! in our hours of ease
> Uncertain, coy, and hard to please,
> And variable as the shade
> By the light quivering aspen made;
> When pain and anguish wring the brow,
> A ministering angel thou!"

In sickness, how thoughtful, how skillful, how gentle a nurse is the true wife! In struggle with temptation or adversity or difficulty, what an inspirer she is! In misfortune or disaster, what lofty heroism does she exhibit and what courage does her bravery kindle in her husband's heart! Instead of being crushed by the unexpected loss, she only then rises to her full grandeur of soul. Instead of weeping, repining and despairing, and thus adding tenfold to the burden of the misfortune, she cheerfully accepts the changed circumstances and becomes a minister of hope and strength. She turns away from luxury and ease to the plainer home, the simpler life, the humbler surroundings, without a murmur. It is in such circumstances and experiences that the heroism of woman's soul is manifested. Many a man is carried victoriously through misfortune and enabled to rise again, because of the strong inspiring sympathy and the self-forgetting help of his wife; and many a man fails in fierce struggle, and rises not again from the defeat of misfortune, because the wife at his side proves unequal to her opportunity.

But a wife's ministry of mercy reaches outside her own doors. Every true home is an influence of blessing in the community where it stands. Its lights shine out. Its songs ring out. Its spirit breathes out. The neighbors know whether it is hospitable or inhospitable, warm or cold, inviting or repelling. Some homes bless no lives outside their own circle; others are perpetually pouring out sweetness and

THE WIFE'S PART

fragrance. The ideal Christian home is a far-reaching benediction. It sets its lamps in the windows, and while they give no less light and cheer to those within, they pour a little beam upon the gloom without, which may brighten some dark path and put a little cheer into the heart of some belated passer-by. Its doors stand ever open with a welcome to everyone who comes seeking shelter from the storm, or sympathy in sorrow, or help in trial. It is a hospice, like those blessed refuges on the Alps, where the weary or the chilled or the fainting are sure always of refreshment, of warmth, of kindly friendship, of gentle ministry of mercy. It is a place where one who is in trouble may go confident ever of sympathy and comfort. It is a place where the young people love to go, because they know they are welcome and because they find there inspiration and help.

And this spirit of the home the wife makes; indeed, it is her own spirit filling the house and pouring out like light or like fragrance. A true wife is universally beloved. She is recognized as one of God's angels scattering blessings as far as her hand can reach. Her neighbors are all blessed by her ministrations. When sickness or sorrow touches any other household, some token of sympathy finds its way from her hand into the shadowed home. To the old she is gentle and patient. To the young she is inciting and helpful. To the poor she is God's hand reached out. To the sufferer she brings strength. To the sorrowing she is a consoler. There is trouble nowhere near but her face appears at the door and her hand brings its benediction.

Some wife, weary already, her hands over-full with the multiplied cares and duties of her household life, may plead that she has no strength to spend in sympathy and help for others. But it is truly wonderful how light these added burdens seem when they are taken up in love. A legend of Elizabeth tells that once she was bearing her cloak full of loaves to the poor whom she daily fed. Her husband met her, and being amazed at the size of the load she bore looked to see what it was, and found only flowers. The loaves were as light as they were fragrant to the noble woman who carried them for the love she bore her Lord. So always the duties we perform out of love for him and his suffering ones become easy and pleasant as we take them up. Heaven's benediction rests ever on the home of her who lives to do good.

Scarcely a word has been said thus far of a wife's personal relation to her husband and the duties that spring out of that relation. These are manifold, and yet they are so sacred and delicate that it seems hardly fit to speak or write of them. A few of the more important of these duties belonging to the wife's part may be merely touched upon.

A true wife gives her husband her fullest confidence. She hides nothing from him. She gives no pledge of secrecy which will seal her lips in his presence. She listens to no words of admiration from others which she may not repeat to him. She expresses to him every feeling, every hope, every desire and yearning, every joy or pain. Then while she utters every confidence in his ear she is most careful to speak in no other ear any word concerning the sacred inner life of her home. Are there little frictions or grievances in the wedded life? Has her husband faults which annoy her or cause her pain? Does he fail in this duty or that? Do differences arise which threaten the peace of the home? In the feeling of disappointment and pain, smarting under a sense of injury, a wife may be strongly tempted to seek sympathy by telling her trials to some intimate friends. Nothing could be more fatal to her own truest interests and to the hope of restored happiness and peace in her home. Grievances complained of outside remain unhealed sores. The wise wife will share her secret of unhappiness with none but her Master, while she strives in every way that patient love can suggest to remove the causes of discord or trouble.

Love sees much in a wife that other eyes see not. It throws a veil over her blemishes; it transfigures even her plainest features. One of the problems of her wedded life is to retain this charm for her husband's eyes as long as she lives, to appear lovely to him even when the color has faded from her cheeks and when the music has gone out of her voice. This is no impossibility; it is only what is done in every true home. But it cannot be done by the arts of the dressmaker, the milliner and the hair-dresser; only the arts of love can do it. The wife who would always hold in her husband's heart the place she held on her wedding day will never cease striving to be lovely. She will be as careful of her words and acts and her whole bearing toward him as she was before marriage. She will cultivate in her own life whatever is beautiful, whatever is winning, whatever is graceful. She will scrupulously avoid whatever is offensive or unwomanly. She will look well to her personal appearance; no woman can be careless in her dress, slatternly and untidy, and long keep her place on the throne of her husband's life. She will look well to her inner life. She must have mental attractiveness. She will seek to be clothed in spiritual beauty. Her husband must see in her ever-new loveliness as the years move on. As the charms of physical beauty may fade in the toils and vicissitudes of life, there must be more and more beauty of soul to shine out to replace the attractions that are lost. It has been said that "the wife should always leave something to be revealed only to her husband, some modest charm, some secret grace, reserved solely for his delight and inspiration, like those flowers which give of their sweetness only to the hand that lovingly gathers them." She should always care more to please him than any other person in the world. She should prize more highly a compliment from his lips than from any other human lips. Therefore she should reserve for him the sweetest

charms; she should seek to bring ever to him some
new surprise of loveliness; she should plan pleasures
and delights for him. Instead of not caring how she
looks or whether she is agreeable or not when no one
but her husband is present, she should always be at
her best for him. Instead of being bright and lovely
when there is company, then relapsing into languor
and silence when the company is gone, she should
seek always to be brightest and loveliest when only
he and she sit together in the quiet of the home.
Both husband and wife should ever bring their best
things to each other.

Again let me say that no wife can over-estimate
the influence she wields over her husband, or the
measure in which his character, his career and his
very destiny are laid in her hands for shaping. The
sway which she holds over him is the sway of love,
but it is mighty and resistless. If she retains her
power, if she holds her place as queen of his life, she
can do with him as she will. Even unconsciously
to herself, without any thought of her responsibility,
she will exert over him an influence that will go far
toward making or marring all his future. If she
has no lofty conception of life herself, if she is vain
and frivolous, she will only chill his ardor, weaken
his resolution and draw him aside from any earnest
endeavor. But if she has in her soul noble womanly
qualities, if she has true thoughts of life, if she has
purpose, strength of character and fidelity to prin-
ciple, she will be to him an unfailing inspiration toward

all that is noble, manly and Christlike. The high
conceptions of life in her mind will elevate his con-
ceptions. Her firm, strong purpose will put vigor
and determination into every resolve and act of his.
Her purity of soul will cleanse and refine his spirit.
Her warm interest in all his affairs and her wise
counsel at every point will make him strong for
every duty and valiant in every struggle. Her
careful domestic management will become an im-
portant element of success in his business life. Her
bright, orderly, happy home-making will be a per-
petual source of joy and peace, and an incentive to
nobler living. Her unwavering fidelity, her tender
affectionateness, her womanly sympathy, her beauty
of soul, will make her to him God's angel indeed,
sheltering, guarding, keeping, guiding and blessing
him. Just in the measure in which she realizes this
lofty ideal of wifehood will she fulfill her mission and
reap the rich harvest of her hopes.

Such is the "woman's lot" that falls on every
wife. It is solemn enough to make her very thought-
ful and very earnest. How can she make sure that
her influence over her husband will be for good, that
he will be a better man, more successful in his career
and more happy, because she is his wife? Not by
any mere moral posturing so as to seem to have lofty
purpose and wise thoughts of life; not by any weak
resolving to help him and be an uplifting inspiration
to him; not by perpetual preaching and lecturing
on a husband's duties and on manly character; she

can do it only by being in the very depths of her soul, in every thought and impulse of her heart and in every fiber of her nature, a true and noble woman. She will make him not like what she tells him he ought to be, but like what she herself is.

So it all comes back to a question of character. She can be a good wife only by being a good woman. And she can be a good woman in the true sense only by being a Christian woman. Nowhere save in Christ can she find the wisdom and strength she needs to meet the solemn responsibilities of wifehood. Only in Christ can she find that rich beauty of soul, that gemming and impearling of the character, which shall make her lovely in her husband's sight when the bloom of youth is gone, when the brilliance has faded out of her eyes and the roses have fled from her cheeks. Only Christ can teach her how to live so as to be blessed and a blessing in her married life.

Nothing in this world is sadder than to compare love's early dreams, what love meant to be, with the too frequent story of the after-life, what came of the dreams, what was the outcome of love's venture. Why so many sad disappointments? Why do so many bridal wreaths fall into dust? Is there no possibility of making these fair dreams come true, of keeping these flowers lovely and fragrant through all the years?

Yes, but only in Christ.

The young maiden goes smiling and singing to the marriage altar. Does she know that if she has not Christ with her she is as a lamb going to the sacrifice? Let her tarry at the gateway till she has linked her life to him, who is the first and the last. Human love is very precious, but it is not enough to satisfy a heart. There will be trials, there will be perplexities, there will be crosses and disappointments, there will be solicitudes and sorrows. Then none but Christ will be sufficient. Without him the way will be dreary. But with his benediction and presence the flowers that droop to-day will bloom fresh again to-morrow, and the dreams of early love will build themselves up into a palace of peace and joy for the solace, the comfort and shelter of old age.

IV

THE PARENTS' PART

IT is a new marriage when the first-born enters the home. It draws the wedded lives together in a closeness they have never known before. It touches chords in their hearts that have lain silent until now. It calls out powers that have never been exercised before. Hitherto unsuspected beauties of character appear. The laughing, heedless girl of a year ago is transformed into a thoughtful woman. The careless, unsettled youth leaps into manly strength and into fixedness of character when he looks into the face of his own child and takes it in his bosom. New aims rise up before the young parents, new impulses begin to stir in their hearts. Life takes on at once a new and deeper meaning. The glimpse they have had into its solemn mystery sobers them. The laying in their hands of a new and sacred burden, an immortal life, to be guided and trained by them, brings to them a sense of responsibility that makes them thoughtful. Self is no longer the center. There is a new object to live for, an object great enough to fill all their life and engross their highest powers. It is only when the children come

that life becomes real, and that parents begin to
learn to live. We talk about training our children,
but they train us first, teaching us many a sacred
lesson, stirring up in us many a slumbering gift and
possibility, calling out many a hidden grace and dis-
ciplining our wayward powers into strong and har-
monious character.

"Children are God's apostles, day by day
    Sent forth to preach of love, of hope, of peace."

Our homes would be very cold and dreary with-
out the children. Sometimes we weary of their
noise. They certainly bring us a great deal of care
and solicitude. They cost us no end of toil. When
they are very young they break our rest many a
weary night with their colics and teethings, and when
they grow older they wellnigh break our hearts many
a time with their waywardness. After they come
to us we may as well bid farewell to living for self
and to personal ease and independence, if we mean
to do faithful duty as parents. There are some who
therefore look upon the coming of children as a
misfortune. They talk about them lightly as "re-
sponsibilities." They regard them as in the way of
their pleasure. They see no blessing in them. But
it is cold selfishness that looks upon children in this
way. Instead of being hindrances to true and noble
living, they are helps. They bring benedictions from
heaven when they come, and while they stay they
are perpetual benedictions.

When the children come what shall we do with them? What duties do we owe to them? How may we discharge our responsibility? What is the parents' part in making the home and the home life? It is impossible to overstate the importance of these questions.

It is a great thing to take these young and tender lives, rich with so many possibilities of beauty, of joy, of power, all of which may be wrecked, and to become responsible for their shaping and training and for the upbuilding of their character. This is what must be thought of in the making of a home. It must be a home in which children will grow up for true and noble life, for God and for heaven. Upon the parents the chief responsibility rests. They are the builders of the home. From them it receives its character, whether good or evil. It will be just what they make it. If it be happy, they must be the authors of the happiness; if it be unhappy, the blame must rest with them. Its tone, its atmosphere, its spirit, its influence, it will take from them. They have the making of the home in their own hands, and God holds them responsible for it.

This responsibility rests upon both the parents. There are some fathers who seem to forget that any share of the burden and duty of making the home-life belongs to them. They leave it all to the mothers. They come and go as if they were scarcely more than boarders in their own house, with no active interest in the welfare of their children. They plead the demands of business as the excuse for their neglect. But where is the business that is so important as to justify a man's evasion of the sacred duties which he owes to his own family? There cannot be any other work in this world which a man can do that will excuse him at God's bar for having neglected the care of his own home and the training of his own children. No success in any department of the world's work can possibly atone for failure here. No piling up of this world's treasures can compensate a man for the loss of those incomparable jewels, his own children.

In the prophet's parable he said to the king, "As thy servant was busy here and there he was gone." May not this be the only plea that some fathers will have to offer when they stand before God without their children: "As I was busy here and there they were gone"? Men are busy in their worldly affairs, busy pressing their plans and ambitions to fulfillment, busy gathering money to lay up a fortune, busy chasing the world's honors and building up a name, busy in the quest for knowledge; and while they are busy their children grow up, and when they turn to see if they are getting on well they are gone. Then they try most earnestly to get them back again, but their intensest efforts avail not. It is too late then to do that blessed work for them and upon their lives which could so easily have been done in their tender years. Dr. Geikie's book, entitled "Life," opens with these words: "Some things God gives often: some he gives only once. The seasons return again and again, and the flowers change with the months, but youth comes twice to none." Childhood comes but once with its opportunities. Whatever is done to stamp it with beauty must be done quickly.

Then it matters not how capable, how wise, how devoted the mother may be; the fact that she does her part well does not free the father in any degree from his share of the responsibility. Duties cannot be transferred. No other one's faithfulness can excuse or atone for my unfaithfulness. Besides, it is a wrong and an unmanly thing for a strong, capable man, who claims to be the stronger vessel, to seek to put off on a woman, whom he calls the weaker vessel, duties and responsibilities which clearly belong to himself. There is a certain sense in which the mother is the real home-maker. It is in her hands that the tender life is laid for its first impressions. In all its education and culture she comes the closer to it. Her spirit makes the home-atmosphere. Yet from end to end of the Scriptures the law of God makes the father the head of the household, and devolves upon him as such the responsibility for the upbuilding of his home, the training of his children, the care of all the sacred interests of his family.

The fathers should awake to the fact that they have something to do in making the life of their own homes besides providing food and clothing and paying taxes and bills. They owe to their homes the best influences of their lives. Whatever other duties press upon them, they should always find time to plan for the good of their own households. The very center of every man's life should be his home. Instead of being to him a mere boarding-house where he eats and sleeps, and from which he starts out in the mornings to his work, it ought to be the place where his heart is anchored, where his hopes gather, to which his thoughts turn a thousand times a day, for which he toils and struggles, and into which he brings always the richest and best things of his life. He should realize that he is responsible for the character and the influence of his home life, and that if it should fail to be what it ought to be, the blame and guilt must lie upon his soul.

Socrates used to say that he wondered how men who were so careful of the training of a colt were indifferent to the education of their own children. Yet even in these Christian days men are found, men professing to be followers of Christ and to believe in the superiority of life itself to all things else, who give infinitely more thought and pains to the raising of cattle, the growing of crops, the building up of business, than to the training of their children. Something must be crowded out of every earnest, busy life. No one can do everything that comes to his hand. But it will be a fatal mistake if any father allows his duties to his home to be crowded out. They should rather have the first place. Anything else had better be neglected than his children. Even religious work in the kingdom of Christ at large must not interfere with one's religious work in the kingdom of Christ in his home. No man is required by the vows and the spirit of his consecration to keep other men's vineyards so faithfully that he cannot keep his own. That a man has been a devoted pastor or a diligent church officer or a faithful Sunday-school superintendent or teacher will not atone for the fact that he was an unfaithful father.

Definitions are important. It will help very greatly in working out the problem of the home-life to settle precisely the object of a home, and what it is intended to accomplish for those who are to grow up in it. Perhaps we say, "A home is a place in which to sleep and get one's meals. It is a place in which to rest when one is tired, to stay and be nursed when one is sick; a place in which to rock the babies and let the children romp and play; a place to receive one's friends and keep the treasures one gathers." Is that all?

The true idea of a home is that it is a place for growth. It is a place for the parents themselves to grow — to grow into beauty of character, to grow in refinement, in knowledge, in strength, in wisdom, in patience, gentleness, kindliness, and all the Christian graces and virtues. It is a place for children to grow — to grow into physical vigor and health and to be trained in all that shall make them true and noble men and women.

If this be the true object and design in setting up a home, the question arises, What sort of home-

culture and home-education will produce these re-
sults? What influences will best fashion human
infancy and childhood into strong, noble manhood
and lovely, queenly womanhood?

For one thing, the house itself in which we live,
with its surroundings and adornments, is important.
Every home influence, even the very smallest, works
itself into the heart of childhood and then reappears
in the opening character. Homes are the real schools
in which men and women are trained, and fathers
and mothers are the real teachers and builders of
life. The poet's song that charms the world is but
the sweetness of a mother's love flowing out in
rhythmic measure through the soul of her child.
The lovely things which men make in their days
of strength are but the reproductions in embodied
forms of the lovely thoughts that were whispered
in their hearts in tender youth. The artist's picture
is but a touch of a mother's beauty wrought out on
the canvas. There is nothing in all the influences
and surroundings of the home of tender childhood so
small that it does not leave its touch of beauty or of
marring upon the life.

Even the natural scenery in which a child is reared
has much to do with the tone and hue of its future
character. Beautiful things spread before the eye
of childhood print themselves on the sensitive heart.
The mountains, the sea, lovely valleys, picturesque
landscapes, forests, flowers, all have their influence
in shaping the life. Still greater is the influence of

the house itself in which a child is brought up. This subject has not yet received the attention which it merits. As people advance in civilization and refinement they build better houses. In great cities the criminal and degraded classes live in wretched hovels. One of the first steps in any wise effort to elevate the low and vicious elements of society must be to provide better dwellings for them. When a whole family are crowded into one room neither physical nor moral health is possible. In a wretched, filthy apartment in a dark court or miserable alley it is impossible for children to grow up into purity and refinement. One of the things for true philanthropy to do is to devise some plan by which better homes may be provided for the poor. Until this is done the leprous spots in our great cities cannot be healed.

In the choosing and preparation of a home the educating power of beauty must not be forgotten. The surroundings should be cheerful and attractive. The house itself, whether large or small, should be neat and tasteful. Its ornaments and decorations should be simple yet chaste and pleasing to the eye. The rooms in which our children are to sleep and play and live we should make just as bright and lovely as our means can make them. If we can afford but two rooms for our home, we should put into them just as much educating power as possible. Children are fond of pictures, and pictures in a house, if they be pure and good, have a wondrous influence in refining their lives. In these days of cheap art, when prints and engravings can be purchased at such small cost, there is scarcely anyone who may not have on the walls of his house some bright bits of beauty which will prove an inspiration to his children. Every home can at least be made bright, clean, sweet and beautiful, even if bare of ornament and decoration. It is almost impossible for a child to grow up into loveliness of character, gentleness of disposition and purity of heart amid scenes of slovenliness, untidiness, repulsiveness and filthiness. But a home clean, tasteful, with simple adornments and pleasant surroundings, is an influence of incalculable value in the education of children.

But the house is not all. Four walls do not make a home, though built of marble and covered with rarest decorations. A family may be reared in a palace filled with the loveliest works of art, and yet the influences may not be such as leave blessing. The home life itself is more important than the house and its adornments. By the home life is meant all the intercourse of the members of the family. It is a happy art, the art of living together in tender love. It must begin with the parents themselves. Unless their life together is loving and true it will be impossible for them to make their home life so. They give the keynote to the music. If their intercourse is marked by bickerings and quarrelings they must expect their children to imitate them. If gentleness and affectionateness characterize their bearing toward each other the same spirit will rule in the family life. For their children's sake, if for no other, parents should cultivate their own lives and train themselves to live together in the most Christlike way. They will very soon learn that good rules and wise counsels from their lips amount to but little unless their own lives give example and illustration of the things thus commended.

We enter some homes, and they are full of sweetness as summer fields are of fragrance. All is order, beauty, gentleness and peace. We enter other homes, where we find jarring, selfishness, harshness and disorder. This difference is not accidental. There are influences at work in each home which yield just the result we see in each. Every home takes its color and tone from its makers. A refined spirit puts refinement into a home, though it be only one plain room without an ornament or a luxury; a coarse nature makes the home coarse, though it be a palace filled with all the elegances that wealth can buy. No home life can ever be better than the life of those who make it. It is nothing less nor more than the spirit of the parents like an atmosphere filling all the house.

What should this home-spirit be? First of all, I would name the law of unselfishness as one of its essential elements. Where selfishness prevails there can be no real happiness. Indeed there is no deep, true and holy love where selfishness rules. As love grows, selfishness dies out in the heart. Love is always ready to deny itself, to give, to sacrifice, just

THE HOME BEAUTIFUL

in the measure of its sincerity and intensity. Perfect love is perfect self-forgetfulness. Hence, where there is love in a home, unselfishness is the law. Each forgets self and lives for the others. But when there is selfishness it mars the joy. One selfish soul will destroy the sweetness of the life of any home. It is like an ugly thorn-bush in the midst of a garden of flowers.

It was selfishness that destroyed the first home and blighted all the loveliness of Paradise; and it has been blighting lovely things in earth's homes ever since. We need to guard against this spirit. Self-culture on the part of the parents is therefore an urgent duty and necessity. Selfishness in them will spread the same unhappy spirit through all the household life. They must be, not in seeming but in reality, what they want their children to be. The lessons they would teach they must live.

Another essential element of true home life is affectionateness; not love only, but the cultivation of love in the daily life of the family, the expression of love in words and acts. This reminder is not altogether needless. There are homes where the love is deep and true; the members of the family would die for each other; when grief or pain comes to one of them the hearts of all the others give out their warmest expressions of affection. There is no question as to the reality and strength of the attachment that binds the household together. Yet in their ordinary intercourse there is a great lack of those exhibitions of kindly feeling which are the sweetest blossomings of love. Husband and wife pass weeks without one of those endearing expressions which have such power to warm the heart. Meals are eaten in haste and in dreary silence, as if the company that surrounded the table had nothing in common and had only been brought together by accident. The simplest courtesies that even polite strangers never fail to extend to each other are altogether omitted in the household intercourse. Ill manners that would not be tolerated for a moment in the ordinary associations of society are oftentimes allowed to find their way into this holiest circle.

This should not be so. The heart's love should be permitted to flow out in word and deed. There are such homes. The very atmosphere as one enters the door seems laden with fragrance. The conversation is bright, sparkling, cheerful, courteous. The warmth of love makes itself felt in continuous influence. No loud, harsh tones are ever heard. A delightful thoughtfulness pervades all the family life. Everyone is watchful of the feelings of the others. There is a respectfulness of manner and bearing that is shown even toward the youngest, toward servants. Without any such sickening extravagances of expression as mark the intercourse of some families, there is here a genuine kindliness of manner which is very charming even to the casual visitor, and which for the hearts of the household has a wondrous warming and satisfying power. All the amenities and courtesies of true politeness are carefully observed, touched also by a tenderness which shows that they are from the heart.

This is the true home spirit. It needs culture. Even the best of us are in danger of growing careless in our own family life. Our very familiarity with our home companions is apt to render us forgetful, and when we have grown forgetful and have dropped the little tendernesses out of our home intercourse, soon the love itself will begin to decay, and what the end may be of coldness and desolateness no one can foretell.

The home life should also be made bright and full of sunshine. The courtesy of the true home is not stiff and formal, but sincere, simple and natural. Children need an atmosphere of gladness. Law should not make its restraints hang like chains upon them. Sternness and coldness should have no place in home life or in family government. No child can ever grow up into its richest and best development in a home which is gloomy and unhappy. No more do plants need sunshine and air than children need joy and gladness. Unhappiness stunts them, so that their sweetest graces never come out.

Whatever parents may do for their children, they should at least make their childhood sunny and tender. Their young lives are so delicate that harshness may mar their beauty forever, and so sensitive that every influence that falls upon them leaves its trace, which grows into the character either as a grace or a blemish. A happy childhood stores away sunshine in the chambers of the heart which brightens the life to its close. An unhappy childhood may so fill the life's fountains with bitterness as to sadden all the after years.

Something must be said concerning the training of children. It is to be kept in mind that the object of the home is to build up manhood and womanhood. This work of training belongs to the parents and cannot be transferred. It is a most delicate and responsible duty, one from which a thoughtful soul would shrink with awe and fear were it not for the assurance of divine help. Yet there are many parents who do not stop to think of the responsibility which is laid upon them when a little child enters their home.

Look at it a moment. What is so feeble, so helpless, so dependent, as a newborn babe? Yet look onward and see what a stretch of life lies before this feeble infant, away into the eternities. Think of the powers folded up in this helpless form, and what the possible outcome may be. Who can tell what skill there may be lying unconscious yet in these tiny fingers, what eloquence or song in these little lips, what intellectual faculties in this brain, what power of love or sympathy in this heart? The parents are to take this infant and nurse it into manhood or womanhood, to draw out these slumbering powers and teach it to use them. That is, God wants a man trained for a great mission in the world, and he puts into the hands of a young father and mother a little babe, and bids them nurse it and train it for him until the man is ready for his mission; or at least to have sole charge of his earliest years when the first impressions must be made, which shall mold and shape his whole career.

When we look at a little child and remember all this, what a dignity surrounds the work of caring for it! Does God give to angels any work grander than this?

Women sigh for fame. They would be sculptors, and chisel out of the cold stone forms of beauty to fill the world with admiration of their skill. Or they would be poets, to write songs to thrill a nation and to be sung around the world. But is any work in marble so great as hers who has an immortal life laid in her hands to shape for its destiny? Is the writing of any poem in musical lines so noble a work as the training of the powers of a human soul into harmony? Yet there are women who regard the duties and cares of motherhood as too obscure and commonplace tasks for their hands. So when a baby comes a nurse is hired, who for a weekly compensation agrees to take charge of the little one, that the mother may be free from such drudgery to devote herself to the nobler and worthier things that she finds to do.

O that God would give every mother a vision of the glory and splendor of the work that is given to her when a babe is placed in her bosom to be nursed and trained! Could she have but one glimpse into the future of that life as it reaches on into eternity; could she look into its soul to see its possibilities; could she be made to understand her own personal responsibility for the training of this child, for the development of its life, and for its destiny, — she would see that in all God's world there is no other work so noble and so worthy of her best powers, and she would commit to no other hands the sacred and holy trust given to her.

This is not the place to present theories of family government; I am trying only to define the parents' part in making the home. So far as their children are concerned, their part is to train them for life, to send them out of the home ready for whatever duty or mission God may have ready for them. Only this much may be said — whatever may be done in the way of governing, teaching or training, theories are not half so important as the parents' lives. They may teach the most beautiful things, but if the child does not see these things in the life of the parent he will not consider them important enough to be adopted in his own life.

What we want to do with our children is not merely to control them and keep them in order, but to implant true principles deep in their hearts which shall rule their whole lives; to shape their character from within into Christlike beauty, and to make of them noble men and women, strong for battle and for duty. They are to be trained rather than governed. Growth of character, not merely good behavior, is the object of all home governing and teaching. Therefore the home-influence is far more important than the home laws, and the parents' lives are of more moment than their teachings.

O mothers of young children, I bow before you in reverence. Your work is most holy. You are fashioning the destinies of immortal souls. The powers folded up in the little ones that you hushed to sleep in your bosoms last night are powers that shall exist forever. You are preparing them for their immortal destiny and influence. Be faithful. Take up your sacred burden reverently. Be sure that your heart is pure and that your life is sweet and clean. The Persian apologue says that the lump of clay was fragrant because it had lain on a rose. Let your life be as the rose, and then your child as it lies upon your bosom will absorb the fragrance. If there is no sweetness in the rose the clay will not be perfumed.

When I think of the sacredness and the responsibility of parents, I do not see how any father and mother can look upon the little child that has been given to them and consider their duty to it, and not be driven to God by the very weight of the burden that rests upon them, to cry to him for help and wisdom. When an impenitent man bends over the cradle of his first-born, when he begins to realize that here is a soul which he must train, teach, fashion and guide through this world to God's bar, how can he longer stay away from God? Let him, as he bends over his child's crib to kiss its sweet lips, ask himself: "Am I true to my child while I shut God out of my own life? Am I able to meet this solemn responsibility of parenthood all alone, in my unaided human weakness, without divine help?" I know not how any father can honestly meet these questions as he looks upon his innocent, helpless child, given to him to shelter, to keep, to guide, and not fall instantly upon his knees and give himself to God.

Let parents be faithful; let them do their best. The work may seem too great for them, and they may faint under its burdens and seem to fail. But what they cannot do the angels will come and finish while they sleep. Night by night they will come and correct the day's mistakes, and if need be do all the poor, faulty work over again. Then at last when the parents sleep in death, dropping out of their hands the sacred work they have been doing for their children, again God's angels will come, take up the unfinished work and carry it on to completeness.

V

THE CHILDREN'S PART

WHAT should the child-life be that would perfectly fulfill its part in the home? We have a model. Once there was a home on earth in which a Child lived whose life was spotless and faultless, and who realized all that is lovely, tender and true in child-life. If we only knew how Jesus lived as a child in that Nazareth home it would help other children to live aright. We know that he helped to make the home happy. He never caused his parents one anxiety, one pang, one moment of shame. He never failed in a duty. We know that he did his part well in the making of that home, and if we only had a memoir of his years of childhood telling us what he did, every other child could study it and imitate his example.

We have no such memoir, but we have one single glimpse into his home life which reveals a great deal. We see him at twelve years of age. He is in the temple at Jerusalem. He has been lost from his parents in the great caravan returning from the passover, and when they find him again we are told in one brief sentence that he went down with them to Nazareth, and was subject unto them. Then for eighteen years longer he remained in that home; we have not another word about him; not another glimpse do we get of him or of his home; Scripture is silent concerning him all those years. We have only this one sentence about the way in which he lived in that home: "He went down with them to Nazareth, and was subject unto them." Yet this one glimpse really reveals the whole history of those years. He was subject to his parents.

Remember who this Child was. It was over his birth that the angels sang their song: "Glory to God in the highest; on earth peace, good will to men." He was the eternal Son of God. He had made all the worlds. He had adorned the heavens. Him all the hosts of glory obeyed. Yet he humbled himself, veiled his glory and dwelt in a lowly home of earth for thirty years. He submitted himself to earthly parents and obeyed them. Then he wrought himself with his own hands to help support the home. No details are given — just this one word; but we can easily fill out the picture for ourselves. We see, for thirty years, from infancy to full manhood, this holy Child exhibiting toward his parents the most perfect dutifulness, obedience, honor and helpfulness. He obeyed them, not by constraint but cheerfully, all these years. He did his part well in the making of that home.

This example is the answer to the question of this

chapter; and what is it but this, that the great duty of childhood in the home life is to obey? He was subject unto them. Although he was the Son of God, yet he learned obedience to human parents. He did their will and not his own. He had entered upon the affairs of his heavenly Father. In the temple he had said, "Wist ye not that I must be about my Father's business?" [1] Yet immediately after saying this he went back to his own home to take and keep for eighteen years more the place of a child. Hence we conclude that the Father's business for him all those years was subjection to his earthly parents. That was the work which was given him to do for that time. He had come to the earth on a great mission, the greatest ever undertaken or performed in the universe, yet the place in which he was prepared for that mission was not in any of the fine schools of the world, but in a lowly home; not at the feet of rabbis and philosophers, but with his own mother for his teacher. What an honor does this fact put upon home! What a dignity upon motherhood!

It would seem that no argument after that was needed to prove to children the duty and the dignity of obedience to parents. We take our place

[1] The Revised Version renders it "in my Father's house," but gives in the margin as the literal rendering "in the things of my Father." Alford says: "Primarily in the house of my Father; but we must not exclude the wider sense, which embraces all places and employments of my Father's."

far back in the history of the world; we stand under the cloud-crowned, fire-wreathed Sinai, and amidst its awful thunderings we hear the voice of God proclaim: "Honor thy father and thy mother; that thy days may be long upon the land which the Lord thy God giveth thee." But even all these scenes of majesty — the voice of Jehovah, the burning mountain, the cloud and the thunder — did not give to this command such sacred authority, such solemn importance, as when Jesus, the Son of God, for thirty years in a lowly home on earth, submitted himself to human parents and obeyed their commands.

Does any question ever arise as to the authority of this divine word in the Decalogue? This picture of Jesus obeying it in that Galilean home is sufficient answer.

Does the thought ever arise, "Is it manly — is it womanly — to yield to my parents, to have no will of my own, to do their bidding in all things?" Behold Jesus till thirty years of age yielding to the control of his human parents, asking them continually what they would have him do, referring every question to them. Was it manly in him? Surely then it cannot be unmanly in any son of earthly parents in this world. Where shall we learn manliness if not in the life and from the example of Jesus? Thomas Hughes says, in speaking of manliness, and of courage as one of its elements: "Tenacity of will lies at the root of all courage, but courage can only rise into true

[81]

manliness when the will is surrendered; and the more absolute the surrender of the will the more perfect will be the temper of our courage and the strength of our manliness." There is nothing manlier in all Christ's life than his quiet subjection to his parents in that cottage at Nazareth, though conscious of his divine origin and nature and of his glorious mission. There is no manlier thing ever seen on this earth than a man in the prime of his strength and power showing deference and love to a humble parent and yielding obedience and honor as if he were a little child.

Does some evil spirit suggest that such subjection to parents keeps one down, puts chains on his freedom, keeps him under restraint and hinders him from rising into grandeur and nobleness of character? Did it have such effect on Jesus? Did the thirty years of submission in his home cramp and fetter his manhood? Did his subjection break his power, repress the glorious aspiration of his soul, stunt and hinder the development of his life and make his career a failure in the end? We know well that it did not. There was a preparation for his mission which, as a man, he could have gotten in no other way but by the discipline he obtained in his own home. No human powers were ever yet cramped or stunted or repressed by taking the place of subjection in a true home. Rather, that life will always be more or less a failure which in its earlier years does not learn to submit and be ruled. No one is fitted for ruling others who has not first learned in his place to obey.

Some one may say again: "My parents are very plain people. They have never known much of the world. They have missed the opportunities that I am enjoying, and therefore have not intelligence or wisdom or education sufficient to direct my life."

We have only to remember again who Jesus was. Was there ever any human parent in this world who was really worthy or capable, in this sense, to be his teacher, to guide and control his life? Was there ever, in any home on earth, such a distance between parents and child as there was in that home at Nazareth? Yet this Son of God, with all his wisdom, his knowledge, his grandeur of character, did not hesitate to submit himself to the training of that peasant mother and that peasant father. Shall any other child, in view of this model child-life at home, assert that he is too far advanced, too much superior in knowledge and culture, too wise and intelligent, to submit to the parents God has given him? If Christ could be taught and trained by his lowly parents for his glorious mission, where is the true parent who is not worthy to be his own child's guide and teacher?

This, then, is the part of every child in the home life. This is the way in which children can do the most to make the home true and happy. It is the part of the parents to guide, to train, to teach, to mold the character. God holds them responsible for this. They must qualify themselves to do it. Then it is the part of the children to accept this guidance, teaching, training and shaping at the parents' hands. When both faithfully do their part the home life will be a sweet song of love; where either fails there will be discordant life, and the angel of blessing will not leave his benison of peace.

Such, in general, is the central feature of the children's part in the home life — to recognize their parents as the head and to yield to them in all things. This is not meant to make them slaves. The home life I am depicting is ruled by love; the parental authority is exercised in love; it seeks only the highest good of each child; it asks nothing unreasonable or unjust. If it withholds things that a child desires, it is either because it is not able to grant them or because the granting of them would work injury rather than benefit. If it seeks to guide the tender feet in a way that is not the chosen way, nor the most easy and pleasant way, it is because a riper wisdom sees that it is the best way. True parental guidance is love grown wise. It is an imitation of God's government. He is our Father and we are his children. We are to obey him absolutely and without question. Yet it is no blind obedience. We know that he loves us with a love deep, tender, unchanging. We know that he is wiser than we, infinitely wiser, and can never err. We know that when he denies a request the granting of it would be an unkindness;

when he leads us in another path than the one we had marked out, his is the right way; when he chastens or corrects there is love in his chastisement or correction. We know that in all his government and discipline he is seeking only our highest good. Our whole duty therefore as God's children is to yield ourselves to his will. True human parenthood is a faint copy of the divine, and to its direction and guidance children are to submit.

This subjection implies obedience to the commands of parents. Thus Paul interprets it: "Children, obey your parents in the Lord; for this is right"; and again, "Children, obey your parents in all things; for this is well-pleasing unto the Lord." It is right on moral grounds, and this ought to settle the matter. True manliness never wants to know more than that a thing is right, is duty. Devotion to duty, at whatever cost, is one of the first elements of heroism. It is right that children should obey their parents, and no further question need be asked, no further reason for obeying need be sought.

But it is also well-pleasing unto the Lord. He is watching how every child acts, and he is well pleased when he sees obedience. This ought to furnish an additional motive, if any were needed. The thought that doing a certain duty faithfully causes emotions of pleasure and approval in the heart of God certainly ought to be a wonderful spur and incentive to heroic fidelity.

This obedience is to extend to "all things," the

things that are agreeable and the things that are disagreeable. Though he may be unjustly treated the child is not to rebel. He may know that his parent is unkind or oppressive, or even cruel, but his duty is not thereby changed. Wrong on the parent's part will never justify wrong on the part of the child. There is only one qualification: children are to obey their parents "in the Lord." If the parent commands the child to commit a sin of course it is not to obey. Herodias was under no moral obligation to obey when her cruel and bloody mother bade her ask for the head of John the Baptist. No human authority is ever binding when it bids us break a divine law. No true parent will knowingly ask anything of his child that is not right; hence the law of parental government requires obedience in all things.

It is told of General Havelock that one day, when a boy, his father, having some business to do, left him on London bridge and bade him wait there till he came back. The father was detained and forgot his son, not returning to the bridge all the day. In the evening he reached home, and after he had rested a little while his wife inquired: "Where's Harry?" The father thought a moment. "Dear me!" said he, "I quite forgot Harry. He is on London bridge, and has been there for eight hours waiting for me." He hastened away to relieve the boy, and found him just where he had left him in the morning, pacing to and fro like a sentinel on his beat. That father knew just where to find his son because he knew that he always obeyed his commands. It is such obedience that pleases God, while it ensures harmony and peace in the home. The parents are the divinely constituted head of the family, and it is the children's part to obey.

This requirement implies also honor and respect. "Honor thy father and thy mother," says the command. Honor is a larger word than obey. We may obey a person whom we do not respect. We are to honor our parents — that is, reverence them — as well as obey them.

There is no need for any argument to prove that every child should honor his parents. Yet it is idle to deny that there is on every hand a lack of filial respect. There are many children who show by their words or acts that their parents are not sacredly enshrined in their hearts.

I heard a bright young girl, well dressed, with good manners and good face, say that her mother looked so old-fashioned that she was ashamed to have her in the parlor or to walk with her on the street. I chanced to know a little about that mother and that daughter. I knew that one reason why the mother looked so old-fashioned, and probably lacked something of refinement of manner, was because of her devotion to the interests of her daughter; she had made a sacrifice of herself for her daughter's sake; she had denied herself in dress and ornament that her daughter might appear well and be admired.

Some young people may read these pages who at times feel as this young girl did. Have you ever sat down quietly to think over and sum up the debt you owe to your old-fashioned mother? Look at the matter for a few moments. Begin with the time when you were a very little baby, as you certainly were once, however great you are now, and think what she had to do for you then. She had to nurse you hour after hour and lie awake many a night to take care of you. Sometimes you were very cross, though you are so gentle now; yet, no matter how cross you were, she was as patient as an angel with you. She wore herself out for you then.

As you grew older she taught you. Did you ever think how little you knew when you came into this world? You had hands and feet and eyes and tongue and brain, but you did not know what they were for or how to use them. It was your loving, patient mother who taught you to walk and to talk and to look and to think.

You have been a great deal of trouble to your mother in your time, but she has borne it all cheerfully for you. She has gone without many things herself that you might have what you wanted. She has worked very hard that you might receive an education and be fitted to shine in society among your friends and be ready for an honored and useful place in this world.

Sometimes you think she looks very plain and old-fashioned. Perhaps she does; perhaps she is more than a little faded and worn; but did you ever think that it is because she has given so much of the best power and energy of her life to caring for you? If she had not chosen to toil and suffer and deny herself for your sake, if she had thought more of herself and less of you, she might have been very much fairer and fresher now. If she had only neglected you instead of herself she might shine now with you in the parlor, for once her cheeks were as lovely as yours are now. She might have found more rest and less hard work if she had not chosen to spend so many hours in stitching away on frocks, trousers, jackets or dresses for you, making new and mending the old. She might have better clothes even now to wear, so that you would not blush to have your friends meet her with you, if she did not take so much interest in dressing you prettily and richly. It may be that the little allowance of money that she gets is not sufficient to dress both herself and you in fashionable array, and that you may be well-clad she wears the same dress and bonnet year after year.

Never forget where your mother lost her freshness and youthful beauty — it was in self-denying toil and suffering for your sake. Those wrinkles in her face, those deep care-lines in her cheeks, that weary look in her eye, — she wears all these marks now where once there was fresh beauty because she has forgotten herself these long years in loving devotion to you. These scars of time and toil and pain are the seals of her care for you.

THE HOME BEAUTIFUL

Look at your father too. He is not so fresh and youthful as once he was. Perhaps he does not dress so finely as some of the young people you see about you or as their fathers dress. There are marks of hard toil upon him, marks of care and anxiety, which in your eye seem to disfigure his beauty. It may be that you blush a little sometimes when your young friends meet you walking with him or when he comes into the parlor when you have company, and wish he would take more pains to appear well. Do not forget that he is toiling these days for you and that his hard hands and his bronzed face are really tokens of his love for you. If he does not appear quite so fresh and handsome as some other men, very likely it is because he has to work harder to give you your pleasant home, your good clothes, your daily food and many comforts, and to send you to school. When you look at him and feel tempted to be ashamed of his appearance just remember this.

Perhaps he is now an old man, with bent form, white hair, slow step, awkward hand, wrinkled face and feeble, broken voice. Forget not what history there is in all these marks that look to you like marrings of his manly beauty. The soul writes its story on the body. The soldier's scars tell of heroisms and sacrifices. The merchant's anxious face and knit brow tell of struggle and anxiety. So gluttony and greed and selfishness and licentiousness write out their record in unmistakable lines on the features, and so do kindness, benevolence, unselfishness and purity.

THE CHILDREN'S PART

You look at your father and see signs of toil, of pain, of self-denial, of care. Do you know what they reveal? They tell the story of his life. He has passed through struggles and conflicts. Do you know how much of this story, if rightly interpreted, concerns you? Is there nothing in the bent form, the faded hands, the lines of care, that tells you of his deep love for you and of sufferings endured, sacrifices made and toils and anxieties for your sake?

When you think thus of what you owe your parents and of what they have borne and wrought for you, can you ever again be ashamed of them? Will not the shame rather be for yourself that you could ever have been so ungrateful as to blush at their homeliness? All the reverence of your soul will be kindled into deepest, purest admiration as you look upon these marks of love and sacrifice for your sake. You will honor them all the more, the more they are worn and wasted, the more they are broken and their grace and beauty shattered. These tokens of self-neglect and self-sacrifice are the jewels in the crown of love.

This honor is not to be shown only by the young child living yet as a child in the old home, but by those who are grown up to full manhood and womanhood. While parents live there never comes a time when a child is no longer a child, owing love and honor. Few things in this world are so beautiful as the sight of a middle-aged man or woman showing true devotion to an aged father or mother. In all the story of the life of President Garfield there is no one incident that will be longer or more tenderly remembered than that little scene on the day of his inauguration, in which he showed such honor to his aged mother. When the last words were spoken and the ceremony was ended; when he was now President of this great nation, and while the huzzas of the vast throngs were falling upon his ear, and when the greatest and noblest of the land were pressing forward to speak their applause, — he turned away from all this, from the cheers of a nation, from the salutations of the great, from the congratulations of foreign ambassadors who bore messages from kings and queens, to give the first thought of that supreme hour to a little aged and worn woman who sat behind him, encircling her with his strong arm and kissing her. It was she to whom he owed all that he was. In the days of poverty she had toiled and suffered for him. She had been both father and mother to him. She had struggled with adversity and had never spared herself that she might bless his early years. She was plain and poor and wrinkled and unfashionable, but she was his mother, and in that hour his loyal, manly heart honored her above all the world. President Garfield will be honored himself in all the future of our country; honored for his noble character and his kingly rank among men; honored for his achievements in the days of war and in the days of peace; honored for the splendor of soul that shone out from his sick room in those long, weary days of death-struggle; but in all the brilliant glory that flashes about his name no one record will shine more imperishably than the sentence that tells how in the moment of his supremest exaltation he bent and printed a kiss of recognition and honor on the wasted face of his mother.

His is not the only case. This noble trait is not so rare as we might think, though it sometimes shines with a luster so brilliant as to draw all eyes to itself. Life's history is not all written. Love's noble deeds are not all wrought in the eyes of the world. Much of the rarest and noblest heroism of love is never seen by human eyes. There are other great men who have shown the same reverence and love for parents in age or feebleness. There are noble daughters, too, who forego the joys offered to them in homes of their own, refusing offers of marriage and voluntarily choosing to live without its blessing and comfort, that they may shelter in old age and surround with love's tenderness the father or the mother, or both, who filled their youth with sunshine. Here and there a heroism finds its way into record; but the noblest heroisms of life, the tenderest histories of love, the most sacred things wrought by human affection, remain unwritten and untold.

Men talk of the wickedness of this world, and surely it is wicked enough. Sin leaves blackness everywhere. There are horrors of ingratitude, of meanness, of shame, of guilt, which make earth a stench in God's nostrils. Yet amid all that is so revolting there are records of such sacred tenderness, such holy beauty, such ineffable love that angels must pause over them in reverence. These are fragments of the Eden loveliness that float down upon the dark tide, like lilies pure and white and unsullied on the black waters of some stagnant bog. In earth's homes where the story of Christ's love has been told, there are filial devotions that are as fair as angelic ministries.

It was on the cross that Jesus paid his last tribute of love and honor to his mother. The nails were in his hands and feet and he hung there in agony. He was dying in deepest shame. The obloquy of the world was pouring its blackest tides upon his head. In the throng below, his eye fell on a little group of loving friends, and among them he saw his mother. Full as his heart was of its own anguish, it was not too full to give thought to her. She would have no protector now. The storms would beat in merciless fury upon her unsheltered head. Besides the bitterness of her bereavement there would be the shame she must endure on his account, the shame of being the mother of one who died on a cross. His heart felt all this, and there, in the midst of his own agony, he made provision for her, preparing a home and shelter for her. Amid the dark scenes of the cross his example shines like a star in the bosom of the blackest clouds, saying to us, "Honor thy father and thy mother."

If true honor for parents has its seat in the heart there is little need for rules or detailed suggestions.

Yet a few particular ways may be mentioned in which children can add to the happiness and blessedness of the home life.

They should show their love for their parents by confiding in them; not simply by believing in them and trusting their love and their wisdom, but by making them the recipients of all their confidences. A wise parent teaches his child from the very beginning to conceal nothing from him, to tell him everything, and there is no part of the child's life in which he takes no interest. True filial love maintains this openness of heart and life toward a parent, even into the years of maturity. There are no other friends in the world who have so much right to all the confidences of children as their own parents. There are no others in whose breasts these confidences will be so safe; they will never betray the trusts that are placed in them by their own children. There are no others who will take such deep interest in all the events of their daily lives. To the true mother nothing is trifling which has interested her child. She listens as eagerly to the story of its experiences, its joys, its disappointments, its plans, its imaginations, its achievements, as other people listen to the recital of some romantic narrative. She never laughs at its fancies nor ridicules anything that it says or does. Then there are no other friends who are such safe and wise counselors. Some one says that bad advice has wrecked many souls and destinies. The advice of godly and loving parents never wrecks souls. Thousands are wrecked because they will not be guided by it, but none by following it. The children that speak every thought, every hope, every ambition, every plan, every pleasure in the ear of their parents and consult them on every matter, will live safely. At the same time they will confer great happiness upon their parents by confiding so fully in them, for it is a great grief to parents when a child does not confide in them and turns away to others with the sacred confidences of his heart.

Children must learn self-denial if they would faithfully do their part. They cannot have everything they desire. They must learn to give up their own wishes for the sake of others. They must learn to do without things that they would like to have. In no other way can home life be made what it should be. Every member of the family must practice self-denial. The parents make many sacrifices for the children, and it is certainly right that the children early learn to practice self-denial to relieve their parents, to help them and to minister to their comfort.

They should also learn thoughtfulness. A home is like a garden of tender plants which are easily broken or bruised. A thoughtless person is forever causing injury or pain, not through intention, but heedlessly. Many, also, who outside are thoughtful, careful of the feelings of others and quick to speak the gentle word that heals and blesses, at home are thoughtless. But surely there is no place in the world where we ought to be so studiously thoughtful as in our own homes. There are no other friends who love us as do the home friends. There are no other hearts that are so much hurt by our want of thought as are the home hearts.

It does not seem unreasonable to expect that even quite young children shall learn to be thoughtful; for those who are older there certainly cannot be a shadow of excuse for rudeness and thoughtlessness. There are in every home abundant opportunities for the culture and display of a thoughtful spirit. Is anyone sick? All the others should avoid noise, moving quietly about the house, speaking softly, so as not to disturb the sufferer. All should be gentle to the invalid, ministering in every little way, brightening the sick room by their kindnesses. This thoughtfulness should show itself also toward parents. Ofttimes they carry heavy burdens while they go about busying themselves in their daily duties. Their work is hard, or they are in ill health, or they are perplexed and anxious, perhaps on their children's account. Bright, happy, joyous youth never can know what burdens rest heavily on the hearts of those who are older, who are in the midst of life's struggles. It would make us gentle even to strangers to know all their secret griefs; much more would it soften our hearts toward our friends to know what trials they have. If children would remember always that their parents have cares, anxieties and sorrows of which they know not it would make them gentle at all times toward them. Here is an opportunity for most helpful ministry, for nothing goes deeper into a parent's heart than the sympathy and gentleness of his own child.

It is not great services that belong to thoughtfulness — only a word of cheer perhaps when one is discouraged, a little tenderness when one looks sad, a little timely help when one is overwrought. It may be nothing more than the bringing of a chair when the father comes in weary, or the running of a little errand for the mother to save her tired feet, or keeping quiet when the baby is sleeping; or it may be only a gentleness of manner and tone showing warmth within. Thoughtlessness causes no end of pain and care, ofttimes of trouble and loss. It goes stalking through heart gardens, treading down the most delicate flowers. It is always saying the wrong word and hurting some one's feelings. It is noisy in the sick room, rude in the presence of sensitive spirits and cold and unsympathetic toward pain and sorrow. It misses the countless opportunities which intimate daily association with others gives to do really kind deeds, to give joy and help, and instead of such a ministry of blessing it is always causing pain. Its confession must continually be "Ah me!

'The wounds I might have healed,
    The human woe and smart!
And yet it never was in my soul
    To play so ill a part.
But evil is wrought by want of thought
    As well as want of heart.'"

"Oh, I did not think," or "I did not mean it," is the poor excuse most common in many homes. It would be better to learn to think, to think of others, especially of those who love us, and then to walk everywhere, but particularly in our own homes, with tender care and regard for the feelings and comfort of others.

Children should early learn to bear some little share in the home work. Instead of being always and only a burden to the loving ones who live and toil and sacrifice for them, they should seek in every way they can to give help. It was Charles Kingsley who said, "We can become like God only as we become of use." There is a deep truth in his words. We begin to live only when we begin to live to minister to others. Instead of singing

"I want to be an angel,"

it were better if the children should strive to be like the angels, and the angels are ministering spirits, sent forth to minister to the heirs of salvation. Home is the school in which we are first to learn and practice the lessons of life. Children should learn there to be useful to their parents and to one another. They can do much in this direction by not requiring unnecessary attendance, by not making trouble and work for others on their account. There are some spoiled children who are such selfish tyrants at home that all the other members of the family are taxed to wait upon them. As soon as possible children should learn to wait upon themselves and in a measure be independent of the help of others, so as to become self-reliant and strong. What more painful picture do we see than that of sons and daughters growing up idle and selfish in their own homes, too indolent to put forth an exertion, too proud to soil their dainty hands with any kind of work, but not too proud to let delicate or already overwrought parents slave to keep them in dainty food or showy array of dress! Nothing good or noble can ever come out of such home life.

Children should make themselves worthy of their parents. They should seek to be all that the father and mother in their most ardent dreams hoped for them. It is a sad thing to disappoint love's brilliant expectations. It matters not so much if mere dreams of earthly greatness fail to come true, for ofttimes the hopes of ambitious parents for their children are only for honors that wither in a day, or for wealth that only sinks the soul to ruin. Such hopes were better disappointed. But in the heart of every true Christian parent there glows an ideal of very fair beauty of character and nobleness of soul, which he wants to see his child attain. It is a vision of the most exalted life, lovelier than that which fills the thought of any sculptor as he stands before his marble and begins to hew at the block; fairer than that which rises in the poet's soul as he bows in ecstatic fervor over his page and seeks to describe his dream. Every true, godly parent dreams of the most perfect manhood and womanhood for his children. He wants to see them grow up into Christlikeness, spotless in purity, rich in all the graces, with character fully developed and rounded out in symmetrical beauty, shining in this world, but shining more and more unto the perfect day.

Just here it may be suggested to children that a large part of what seems to them "fussiness" and needless faultfinding on the part of parents is due to anxiety to have them perfect. Parents sometimes err through over-anxiety or through unwise and irritating because incessant admonitions, but the sons and daughters should recognize the fact that deep anxiety for their well-doing is at the root of even this excessive carefulness.

There is a story of a great sculptor weeping like a child as he stood and looked on the fragments of his breathing marble, the work of his lifetime and his ripest powers, the dream of his fairest hopes, which lay now shattered at his feet. With still deeper sorrow and bitterer grief do true and godly parents look upon the wreck of their high hopes for their children and the shattering of the fair ideals that glowed in their hearts during the bright years of childhood and youth.

If children would do their part well in return for all the love that has blessed their helpless years and surrounded them in their youth, and that lingers still unwasted in the days of manhood and womanhood, they must seek to realize in their own lives all the sacred hopes of their parents' hearts. A wrecked and debauched manhood or a frivolous and purpose-less womanhood is a poor return for parental love, fidelity and sacrifice. But a noble life, a character strong, true, earnest and Christlike, brings blessed and satisfying reward to a parent for the most toil-some and painful years of self-forgetting love. Parents live in their children, and children hold in their hands the happiness of their parents. Let them never be untrue to their sacred trust. Let them never bring down the gray hairs of father or mother with sorrow to the grave. Let them be worthy of the love, almost divine, that holds them in its deathless grasp. Let them so live as to be a crown of honor to their parents in their old age. Let them fill their declining years with sweetness and tenderness. Let them make a pillow of peace for their heads when death comes.

When our parents grow old they exchange places, as it were, with us. There were years when we were feeble and helpless, unable to care for ourselves; then they cared for us. They watched over us; they toiled and sacrificed for us; they sheltered us from hardship and trial; they threw around our tender years love's sweetest gentleness and holiest protection. Now we are strong and they are feeble; we are able to endure hardship and toil, but the faintest breath of storm makes them tremble and the lightest toil wearies them. This is the time for us to repay them. It is ours now to show tenderness to them, to shelter them from trial and to pour about them as much of love's tenderness as possible.

VI

BROTHERS AND SISTERS

WHAT should be the home intercourse of brothers and sisters? What should they do toward the home life? How should they live together? These questions may be answered in general by saying that a close and tender friendship should exist between them. This sounds like a very commonplace remark. Of course brothers and sisters should be friends, and should live together in an intimate relationship as friends. No one denies it. But do we universally find this warm, living and tender friendship where there are young people in a home? We often find strong ties and attachments, mutual affection and interests, and much that is very beautiful; but when we come closer and look for friendship in the true sense, it is wanting. The brothers and sisters may love one another very truly, but they seek their friends outside the home. They go outside for warm sympathy, for close intimacy, for confidential companionship.

It is not hard to find reasons for this. Living always together and knowing one another from infancy, members of the same family are apt to grow uninteresting to one another. The sameness of the society, day after day, takes away its freshness. The common life which they all lead under the same roof, with the same pursuits, the same topics for conversation, the same incidents and experiences, the same hopes and fears, the same joys and sorrows, the same books, the same social life, renders it difficult for the members of a household to impress one another in continual repetition and ever freshly kindle inspiration and emotion the one in the other, as friends from other homes can do, coming in only now and then.

Then the fact that it is home and that the ties are natural and thought to be secure; that the members are sure of each other, without making any effort to win confidence and regard; that love between them is a matter of course, as if by nature, without winning it or cherishing it or troubling themselves to keep it, — this is another of the causes for the absence of real friendship among brothers and sisters. They imagine that family affection is a sort of instinct, not subject to the laws which control other affections; that it does not need to be sought or gained or won, as affection must be in others, by giving affection in return and by the countless little tendernesses and thoughtfulnesses which are shown to others whom they desire to win. They forget that the principle, "He that hath friends must show himself friendly," applies in the family just as well as outside of it.

They forget that friendship anywhere must be cherished or it will die; that indifference and coldness will cause it to wither as drought causes summer flowers to wither. They imagine, in a word, that the love of the family is so sure and strong that it needs no care, no pains, to keep it safe. So it is that in very many homes brothers and sisters come and go, day after day, and year after year, mingling in all the life of the household, but never really forming close friendships among themselves.

Friendships in the family require care and culture as do other friendships. We must win one another's love inside the home doors just as we win the love of outside friends. We must prove ourselves worthy; we must show ourselves unselfish, self-forgetful, thoughtful, kind, tender, patient, helpful. Then when we have won each other we must keep the treasure of affection and confidence, just as we do in the case of friends not in the sacred circle of home.

If we have a friend whom we respect and prize very highly, we all know at what pains we are to retain his friendship. We are not sure of it regardless of our treatment of him. We are most careful never to do anything to make us seem unworthy of the friendship. We try to prune from our own character anything that would displease our friend. We cultivate assiduously those qualities of heart and life which he admires. We watch for opportunities to do kindnesses and show favors to him. We guard against whatever would wound him or cause him pain.

We give him our confidence, we trust him and prove our affection for him in countless ways.

Let no one suppose that home friendships can be won and kept in any other way. We cannot depend on nature or instinct to do this for us. We must live for each other. We must gain each other's heart by giving just what we expect to receive. We must cherish the friendship that we have won. Unless we do, it will not grow. We must watch our words and our conduct. We must seek to please and take pains never to wound or grieve. We must deny self and live for one another. We must confide in one another. We must cultivate in our own hearts and lives whatever is beautiful, whatever is tender, whatever is holy, whatever is true. Friendships in our own home, to be deep and true and heart-satisfying, must be formed by the patient knitting of soul to soul and the growing of life into life, just as in other friendships.

Is it thus in most of our homes? There are distinguished exceptions; there are homes which shine like bits of heaven dropped down upon this sin-cursed earth. In these, natural affection has grown into a holy web of real and sacred friendship, binding brothers and sisters in closest bonds. There are brothers who have no friends so close as their own sisters; there are sisters who confide and trust in their own brothers as in no other friends.

One of the tenderest as well as saddest stories of all literature is that of Charles and Mary Lamb. In a fit of insanity the sister had taken the life of her own mother. All her life after this she was subject to periods of frenzy, when it was necessary for her to be confined in an asylum. Then it was that her brother's affection showed itself. He lived for his sister in unselfish devotion. When she was in her right mind she lived with him, and he watched over her with a care that was most touching.

When the fit of insanity was coming on there were premonitory symptoms; they would then start off together for the asylum where for a time she must be confined. One of their friends relates how on one occasion he met the brother and sister weeping bitterly as hand in hand they slowly paced together a little footpath across the fields, and joining them he found that they were taking their solemn way to the accustomed asylum. This was not something that occurred once or twice only, but frequently, and was liable to occur at any time; it was not for a year or two only, but for thirty-five years, until death separated them. He "did not nerve himself to bear his awful charge for a month or for a year; he endured his cross through life, conscious that there was no escape from its burden and from its pains." The indescribable pathos of this story is equaled only by the matchless devotion and constancy of the brother to his sister in all her sad and terrible lot and by her tender, all-absorbing affection for him.

The history of life is not all written. Here and there in many a quiet home there is a friendship between brother and sister, on which God's angels look with' admiring love, which realizes all that is tender and beautiful in human attachment and affection. Yet I do not think I write a rash word when I say that such friendships are rare. Ofttimes the intercourse of brothers and sisters in the home lacks even the graces of ordinary civility. As soon as the door shuts them within, restraint is thrown off, selfishness comes to the surface, courtesy is laid aside. There is no pleasant conversation. Neither lives for or tries to please the other. The speech is rude or careless and the whole bearing cold or indifferent. The better nature is hidden and the worse comes to the surface. Instead of a tender idyl of grace and beauty the intercourse of brother and sister is a harsh and painful discord. It should not be so. Brothers and sisters should live together as intimate friends, should carefully win and sedulously keep each other's love, dwelling together in unity and tender affection. There is no friendship in the world so pure, so rich and helpful, as that of the family, if only it be watched and tended as it should be.

Why should not a brother make a confidante of his own sister rather than of any other? Why should not a sister look to her own brother for counsel, for protection, for advice, for intimacy, rather than to any other? Why should not brothers be proud to have their own sisters lean upon their arms? and why should not sisters be proud to look up into the faces of their brothers, and feel secure in the shelter of their manly love? But instead of this what do we often see? The brothers turn away from their own homes to find their companionships and friendships in other circles. As if their own sisters were not worthy of them, or it were a shame for a young man to devote himself in any measure to his sisters, as soon as they are old enough to be their companions they begin to seek other friendships. The sisters are then left to go unprotected or to accept that courtesy and shelter from others which their own brothers have failed to give.

That is the picture as too often it is. What it ought to be, however, is different.

A young man should be more polite to his own sister than to any other young woman under heaven; and a young woman should ever turn to her brother as the one nearest in all this world to her until a husband stands by her side.

Brothers and sisters are each other's natural keepers. If they fulfilled their duties in this regard, the one to the other, life would show fewer wrecks. They should shield each other. They should be an inspiration to each other in the direction of all noble thought and better life. They should be each other's guardian angels in this world of danger and of false and fatal paths.

Sisters may be their brothers' angels. There is a picture of a child walking on a path that is covered with flowers. Along the edge of the narrow way is shrubbery which hides from the child's sight a deep precipice. The child is unconscious of danger, charmed by the flowers and not seeing how one mis-step would hurl it to death. Over the little pilgrim's head hovers a shadowy angel form, scarcely visible, but with eager, loving interest in his eye, while his hand gently touches the child's shoulder; his mission is to guide the child's steps, to shield it from danger and to keep it from falling. The picture represents a truth in the loving providence of God. There are angels who guard, guide, shelter and keep God's children. They are ministering spirits. They keep us in all our ways. Over each one of us a guardian angel hovers unseen evermore. But there is also a most blessed angel ministry of sisters in behalf of their brothers. There is no need to paint here any picture of the perils to which young men are exposed in this world. It makes the heart bleed to see how many of the noblest of them are destroyed, dragged down to ruin, their fair lives blackened, their godlike manhood debauched. They go out of the home pure, with lofty aspirations, with high hopes, with brilliant promises, challenging the admiration of all who know them; they come back, how often! stained, degraded, hopes wrecked, promises unfulfilled. Every young man who enters life enters a fierce battle in which no truce will come till he either lies down in final defeat or wins the last victory and enters into joy and rest. Life is hard. The young enter it without thought, without anxiety, without serious or solemn sense of danger, because they are not conscious of its true meaning. But it is one prolonged struggle with enemies and with perils.

To every young man life is specially hard. As he goes into it he needs the sympathy of all who love him; he needs the prayers and the help of all his friends. For want of the strong support of love many a young man goes down in the battle, and many who come through victorious owe their victories to the holy affection of truly loyal hearts that inspired them with hope and courage in all their hours of struggle. The value of strong friendships never can be known in this world.

Next to mother and father there is no one who can do so much to help a young man to live nobly as his own sister. She cannot always go with him. Her weak arm could not always shield him if she were beside him. But there is a help which she can give him that will prove mightier than her presence. It is not the help of good advice and earnest words — these should have power, too — but the help rather of silent and holy influence, gained in the home by a life of unselfishness and beauty, and then held as a potent charm outside and beyond the home walls. There is a power over her brother possible to every true sister, which would be like the very hand of God to guide him and restrain him in all the paths of life. All sisters, however, do not have this power over their brothers, and, alas! sometimes the power is for evil rather than for good.

May I try to tell you, dear girls, how you can

indeed be your brothers' guardian angels? Show them in your own lives at home the perfect grace and beauty of a true, noble and lofty womanhood. Strive after all that is delicate, all that is pure, all that is tender, all that is holy and sacred in the divine ideal of woman. Show them in yourselves such perfect loveliness that they will turn away ever after from everything that is unlovely. Make virtue so attractive to them, as they see it embodied in you, that they will always be repelled by vice. Let them see in you such purity of soul, such sweetness of spirit, such divine sanctity, that wherever they go your influence will hang about them like an armor of defense, or, like an angel, hover above their heads in perpetual benediction. Be as nearly a perfect woman, each one of you, through Christ's help, as it is possible for you to be. Then when temptations come to your brother there will rise up before his eyes such visions of purity and love that he will turn away with loathing from the tempter.

But oh! if you are not such angels of true womanhood to your brothers, if you do not fill their souls with visions of purity and sweetness, what help do you hope to be to them when they stand in the face of sore temptations? If you are deceitful, if you are selfish, if you are false, if you violate the holy proprieties of modesty and true refinement; if you are frivolous and trifling; if you follow pleasure, turning away from everything serious; if you are careless or heartless, — do not deceive yourselves with the vain hope that you can be in any high sense your brothers' guardians in the day of danger. You may advise, you may persuade, you may implore with tears and every token of tender love, when they begin to yield, but your entreaties will avail nothing because your own life has failed to stand the test and to exhibit before them a lofty ideal of womanhood. But if you will only be true, noble, unselfish, gentle, womanly, in the highest, purest sense; if you only are thoughtful and considerate and live for a purpose, making your character decided and strong, you will throw over your brothers a silent, imperceptible yet mighty influence, which will be a shield to them in danger, a panoply in temptation, and which will fill their hearts with the purest, loftiest aspirations and aims.

Brothers should also be their sisters' guardians. Every young man knows what true gallantry is, and what it requires of him. He is to honor every lady, whether rich or poor, whether of higher or lower station, and show her every respect. He is to be to every woman a true knight, ready to defend her from danger, to shield her from every insult, to risk his own life in her behalf. There is no better test of a gentleman than his treatment of women.

Now, to whom ought every young man to show the highest, truest gallantry? To whom ought he first of all to be a most true and loyal knight? To whom if not to his own sisters? Do not they come first in the circle of those to whom he owes honor? Have they not the first claim on his affection? If he is not a true gentleman to his own sisters, can he be at heart a true gentleman to any other woman? Can a young man be manly, and treat his own sisters with less respect and honor than he treats other young ladies? Hence a still higher test of a gentleman is his treatment of his own sisters. His chivalry must show itself first toward those who are closest to him in natural ties. He must show them the truest deference. He must treat them with that delicate regard, that gentle, affectionate respect, that tells of the loftiest gallantry. He must consider himself their true knight, whose office it is to throw about them every needed shelter, to serve them, and to promote their highest good in every way.

Of course there is no young man with one spark of the honor of true manliness in his breast who will not instinctively defend his sister, if she is insulted in the street. He will put himself instantly between her and the danger. Neither is there any brother worthy of the name who will not defend the honor of his sister if vile tongues asperse it. But more than this is required of a loyal brother. He should make himself a wall about his sister to shield her from every evil and unholy influence. Every young man knows other young men; he knows their character, their habits, their good and evil qualities. He knows the young men whose lives are impure, who are licentious, who consort with harlots. He knows those who indulge in strong drink, those who are godless and profane, those whose lives are stained with the filth of debauchery. Can he be a true brother and permit such a young man to be the companion of his pure and gentle sister? Can he allow her in the innocence of her heart to accept the attentions of such a young man, to lean upon his arm, to look up into his face with trust? Can he allow her to give her soul's confidences to him? Can he see a friendship forming, strengthening, between his sister and such a young man and remain silent, uttering in her ear no voice of warning or protest, and yet be a loyal and faithful brother to her?

This is a place for plain, strong and earnest words. Surely young men do not think of this matter seriously or they would require no argument to convince them of their duty. Put the case in the strongest possible form and bring it close home. You have a sister pure as a lily. She has grown up beside you in the shelter of the home. Her eyes have never looked upon anything vile. Her ears have never heard an impure word. Her soul is white as the snowflakes that fall from the clouds. You love her as you love your own life. You honor her as if she were a queen. A young man seeks to win her regard and confidence. He stands well in society, has good manners, is attractive, intelligent. But you know that he frequents resorts of evil, that his secret life is unchaste, that his soul is stained with low and vile sins, that he is the victim of habits which will bring ruin and dishonor in the end. Your sister knows nothing of his true character. Can you permit him to become her companion? Are you not bound to tell her that he is not worthy of her? Can you do otherwise and be a faithful brother?

Besides this standing between his sister and danger every brother should also show her in his own life the ideal of the truest, purest, most honorable manhood. If it be true that the best shield a sister can make for her brother is to show him in herself the loftiest example of womanhood, it is true also that the truest defense a brother can make for his sister is a noble manhood in his own person. He must exhibit before her continually a character without spot or stain, with high aspirations, with generous sympathies, with pure, true, unselfish, Christlike spirit and disposition. If he is going to shield his sister from the impure, he must not be impure himself. He must show her in himself such a high ideal of manhood that her soul shall unconsciously and instinctively shrink from everything that is vulgar, rude or evil. There is no other defense so perfect. Let no brother think that he can be a shelter from evil to his sister if his own life be not unsullied and true.

There is no better place than this to say a few earnest words to young girls on the cultivation of their own hearts. Among all the elements of beauty in the character of a young woman none is more essential than purity of mind and heart, and none gives such grace to the whole life and spirit. It is not possible even to think of true womanhood without purity. It were as easy to think of a rose without beauty or of a lily without whiteness. Amid the wreck of this world, wrought by sin, there are still some fragments of the beauty of Eden, and among these none is lovelier than the unsullied delicacy of a true woman's heart. It is possible, too, to preserve this holy purity even amid all this world's sin and foulness. I have seen a lily floating in the black waters of a bog. All about it lay stagnation and vileness, but in the midst of all this the lily remained pure as the robes of an angel. It lay on the dark pond, rocked on the bosom of every ripple, yet never receiving a stain. It held up its unsullied face toward God's blue heaven and poured its fragrance all about it. So is it possible, even in this world of moral evil, for a young woman to grow up, keeping her soul unstained in the midst of it all and ever breathing out the perfume of holy, unselfish love.

There is need here for earnest warning. There are dangers to which every young girl is exposed. There are indications in society of the lowering of the tone of girlhood. There are things in some circles that are painful to every sensitive heart. There are papers and books offered everywhere, and read by too many, which leave a trail of stain on the fair flowers of maidenly refinement. When on a winter's morning you breathe upon the exquisite tracery of frostwork on a window-pane, it melts down, and no human hand can ever restore it. Still less is it possible to restore the charm of purity to the soul that has lost it. If a young girl would grow into the most spotless womanhood, radiant in every feature with the loveliness of Christ's own image, she must from her earliest youth, through all the experiences of her life, maintain unsullied purity of heart.

So far the duty only of brothers to sisters and sisters to brothers has been considered. It ought to make a young man's heart exult to have a beautiful and noble sister to lean upon his arm and look up to him for protection, for counsel, for strong, holy friendship. And a sister ought to be proud and happy to have a brother growing into manly strength, to stand by her side, to bear her upon his arm, and to shelter her from life's storms. Between brother and sister there should be a friendship deep, strong, close, confiding and faithful.

But the home presents opportunities also for friendships between brother and brother, and between sister and sister. Why should not the brothers of a family stand together? They have common ties, common joys and sorrows, common interests. The same mother gave them birth and taught their infant lips to lisp the words of prayer. The same father toiled and sacrificed for them. The same home roof shelters them. Why should they not be to each other the loyalest of friends? When one is in trouble, to whom should his instincts teach him first to turn if not to his own brother? Where should he think to find quicker sympathy and readier help than in his brother's heart and hand? Who should be so willing to give help as a brother?

Yet, do we always find such friendship between brothers? Sometimes we do. There are families of brothers who do stand together in most loyal affection. They share each other's burdens. If one is in trouble the others gather close about him with strong sustaining sympathy, as when one branch of a tree is bruised all the other branches give of their life to restore the one that is injured. The picture is very beautiful, and it is what should be seen in every home in which brothers dwell. But too often it is not seen. Frequently they drift apart even while they stay under the home roof. Each builds up interests of his own. They seek different friends outside. Sometimes over a father's grave they quarrel about petty questions of property, and unholy feuds build walls between hearts and lives that should have been bound together inseparably forever. With so much in common, with the most sacred ties to bind them together, and the most holy memories to sanctify their union, brothers should permit nothing ever to estrange them from each other. No selfish interest, no question of money or property, no bitterness or feud, should ever come in to sever their hearts. Though continents divide them and seas roll between them, their love should remain faithful, strong and true forever.

In like manner the sisters in a home should maintain their friendship for each other through all the changes and all the varied experiences of life. This they do more frequently than their brothers. There are many very beautiful sisterly attachments. Their life within the home holds them together more closely than brothers are held in their outside life. They have better opportunities for the cultivation of friendship among themselves in the many hours they sit together at their household work. Then the interests of their lives are less likely to separate them or start differences between them. Nothing is lovelier than the picture of sisters locked in each other's arms, their lives blending in holy love, the one helping the other, giving comfort in sorrow, strength in weakness and help in trial.

Are the brothers and sisters who read these pages realizing in their own lives the ideals which have here been even so imperfectly sketched? Are they living together in tender love in their own home? If they are, heaven's benediction will fall upon their hearts and lives like a baptism of holy peace. If they are not, where is the fault? What can be done to correct it? Too many blessed possibilities of joy, of love and of helpfulness lie in these sacred relationships to be neglected or ruthlessly tossed into the dust. Life is too short to be spent in strife and discord anywhere, especially in the holy circle of the home. Strifes and alienations here are the seeds for a harvest of sorrow. Sad, sad will it be to stand by the coffin of a brother or a sister, and while we look at the cold, silent clay, remember that we were ever unkind to one who stood so near, that we ever failed in acts of love, or that we ever allowed anything to estrange us or make our intercourse cold and formal.

Is your home plain and bare? Must you meet hardships and endure toil? Have you cares and privations? Do you sigh for something finer, more beautiful, less hard? Call up love to wreathe itself over all your home life. Cultivate home friendships. Bind up the broken home ties. Plant the flowers of affection in every corner. Then soon all will be transfigured. You will forget care, hardships and toil, for they will all be hidden under lovely garments of affection. Your eye will see no more the homeliness, the hardness, the anxieties, the toils, but will be charmed with the luxuriance of love that shall cover every blemish.

VII

THE HOME LIFE

THERE is nothing insignificant in the life that we live within our own doors. There is nothing that is without influence in the building up of character. On some old rocks the geologist shows you the tracks of birds made ages and ages ago, and the print of the leaf that fell or the dents made by the pattering raindrops. It was soft sand then, but it hardened afterwards into rock, and these marks were preserved, imperishable records of the history of a day that shone uncounted centuries ago. Let no one think that the history of any day in the life of a home is recorded any less imperishably on the sensitive lives of the children.

There is something infinitely more important than the mere performance of duties. There is an unconscious influence that hangs about every life like an atmosphere, which is more important than the words or acts of the life. There are many parents who fail in no duty, who are deeply anxious for their children and really strive to make their home what it should be, whose influence is not a benediction. When the results of life are all gathered up it will probably be seen that the things in us which have made the deepest and most lasting impressions in our homes and upon our children have not been the things we did with purpose and intention, planning to produce a certain effect, but the things we did when we were not thinking of training or influencing or affecting any other life. A wise writer says: "I look with wonder on that old time, and ask myself how it is that most of the things I suppose my father and mother built on especially to mold me to a right manhood are forgotten and lost out of my life. But the things they hardly ever thought of — the shadow of blessing cast by the home, the tender, unspoken love, the sacrifices made and never thought of, it was so natural to make them, ten thousand little things so simple as to attract no notice and yet so sublime as I look back at them, — they fill my heart still, and always with tenderness when I remember them, and my eyes with tears."

It is not so much strict fidelity in teaching and training that is powerful in our homes for holy impression as it is the home life itself. The former is like the skillful trimming and training of a vine; the latter is like the sunshine and the rain that fall upon the vine. The writer above quoted adds: "It is said that a child, hearing once of heaven, and that his father would be there, replied, 'Oh! then I dinna want to gang.' He did but express the instinct of a child to whom the father may be all that is good

THE HOME BEAUTIFUL

except just goodness; and be all that any child can
want except what is indispensable — that gracious
atmosphere of blessing in the healing shadow it
casts, without which even heaven would come to be
intolerable."

It is necessary that the whole home life and home
spirit should be in harmony with the teaching and
training, if these are to make holy impressions.
Simple goodness is more important than the finest
theories of home government most thoroughly and
faithfully carried out. There is nothing in the daily
routine of the family life that is unimportant. In-
deed, it is ofttimes the things we think of as without
influence that will be found to have made the deepest
impression on the tender lives of the household.

Few things are more important in a home than its
conversation, and yet there are few things to which
less thought is given. The power to communicate
good which lies in the tongue is simply incalculable.
It can impart knowledge, utter words that will shine
like lamps in darkened hearts, speak kindly sentences
that will comfort sorrow or cheer despondency,
breathe out thoughts that will arouse and quicken
heedless souls, even whisper the secret of life-giving
energy to spirits that are dead.

The good we could do in our homes with our
tongues if we would use them to the utmost limit
of their capacity it is simply impossible to compute.
Why should so much power for blessing be wasted?
Especially why should we ever pervert these gifts

and use our tongues to do evil, to give pain, to scatter seeds of bitterness? It is a sad thing when a child is born dumb, but it were better far to be dumb and never to have the gift of speech at all, than, having it, to employ it in speaking only sharp, unloving or angry words.

The home conversation should be loving. Home is the place for warmth and tenderness. Yet there is in many families a great dearth of kind words. In some cases there is no conversation at all worthy of the name. There are no affectionate greetings in the morning or good-nights at parting when the day closes. The meals are eaten in silence. There are no fireside chats over the events and incidents of the day. A stranger might mistake the home for a deaf and dumb institution. In other cases it were better if silence reigned, for only words of miserable strife and shameful quarreling are heard from day to day. Husband and wife, who vowed at the marriage altar to cherish the one the other till death, keep up an incessant petty strife of words. Parents who are commanded in the holy word not to provoke their children to anger lest they be discouraged, but to bring them up in the nurture of the Lord, scarcely ever speak gently to them. They seem to imagine that they are not "governing" their children unless they are perpetually scolding at them. They fly into passions against them at the smallest irritation. They issue their commands to them in words and tones which would better suit the despot of some petty savage tribe than the head of a Christian household. It is not strange that under such "nurture" the children, instead of dwelling together in unity, with loving speech, should only wrangle and quarrel, speaking only bitter words in their intercourse with one another. That there are many homes of just this type it is idle to deny. That prayer is offered morning and evening in these families only makes the matter worse, as it is mockery for a household to rise from their knees only to begin another day of strife and bitterness.

Nothing in the home life needs to be more carefully watched and more diligently cultivated than the conversation. It should be imbued with the spirit of love. No bitter word should ever be spoken. The language of husband and wife in their intercourse together should always be tender. Anger in word, or even in tone, should never be suffered. Chiding and faultfinding should never be permitted to mar the sacredness of their speech. The warmth and tenderness of their hearts should flow out in every word that they utter to each other. As parents, too, in their intercourse with their children, they should never speak save in words of Christlike gentleness. It is a fatal mistake to suppose that children's lives can grow up into beauty in an atmosphere of strife. Harsh, angry words are to their sensitive souls what frosts are to the flowers. To bring them up in the nurture of the Lord is to bring them up as Christ himself would, and surely that would be with infinite gentleness. The blessed influence of loving speech, day after day and month after month, it is impossible to estimate. It is like the falling of warm spring sunshine and rain on the garden, causing lovely flowers to spring up in every nook and corner, and filling all the air with sweet fragrance. Only beauty and gentleness of character can come from such a home.

But home conversation needs more than love to give it its full influence. It ought to be enriched by thought. The Saviour's warning against idle words should be remembered. Every wise-hearted parent will seek to train his household to converse on subjects that will yield instruction or tend toward refinement. The table affords an excellent opportunity for this kind of education. Three times each day the family gathers there. It is a place for cheerfulness. Simply on hygienic grounds meals should not be eaten in silence. Bright, cheerful conversation is an excellent sauce and a prime aid to digestion. If it prolongs the meal, and thus appears to take too much time out of the busy day, it will add to the years in the end by increased healthfulness and lengthened life. In any case, however, something is due to refinement, and still more is due to the culture of one's home life. The table should be made the center of the social life of the household. There all should appear at their best. Gloom should be banished. The conversation should be bright and sparkling. It should consist of something besides dull and threadbare commonplaces. The weather is a worn-out topic. The idle gossip of the street is scarcely a worthy theme for such hallowed moments.

The conversation of the table should be of a kind to interest all the members of the family; hence it should vary to suit the age and intelligence of those who form the circle. The events and occurrences of each day may with profit be spoken of and discussed, and now that the daily newspaper contains so full and faithful a summary of the world's doings and happenings, this is easy. Each one may mention the event which has specially impressed him in reading. Bits of humor should always be welcome, and all wearisome recital and dull, uninteresting discussion should be avoided.

Table-talk may be enriched, and at the same time the intelligence of all the members of a family may be advanced, by bringing out at least one new fact at each meal, to be added to the common fund of knowledge. Suppose there are two or three children at the table ranging in their ages from five to twelve. Let the father or the mother have some particular subject to introduce during the meal which will be both interesting and profitable to the younger members of the family. It may be some historical incident, or some scientific fact, or the life of some distinguished man. The subject should not be above the capacity of the younger people for whose especial benefit it is introduced, nor should the conversation be overladen by attempting too much at one time.

One single fact clearly presented and firmly impressed is better than whole chapters of information poured out in a confused jargon on minds that cannot remember any part of it. A little thought will show the rich outcome of a system like this if faithfully followed through a series of years. If but one fact is presented at every meal, there will be a thousand things taught to the children in a year. If the subjects are wisely chosen the fund of knowledge communicated in this way will be of no inconsiderable value. A whole system of education lies in this suggestion, for besides the communication of important knowledge, the habit of mental activity is stimulated, interest is awakened in lines of study and research which afterwards may be followed out, tastes are improved, whilst the whole effect upon the family life is elevating and refining.

It may be objected that such a system of table-talk could not be conducted without much thought and preparation on the part of parents. But if the habit once were formed and the plan properly introduced it would be found comparatively easy for parents of ordinary intelligence to maintain it. Books are now prepared in great numbers giving important facts in small compass. Then there are encyclopedias and dictionaries of various kinds. The newspapers contain every week paragraphs and articles of great value in such a course. A wise use of scissors and paste will keep scrapbooks well filled with materials which can readily be made available.

It will be necessary to think and plan for such a system, to choose the topics in advance and to become familiar with the facts. This work might be shared by both parents, and thus be easy for both. That it will cost time and thought and labor ought not to be an objection, for is it not worth almost any cost to secure the benefits and advantages which would result from such a system of home instruction?

These are hints only of the almost infinite possibilities of good which lie in the home conversation. That so little is realized in most cases where so much is possible is one of the saddest things about our current life. It may be that these suggestions though crude, may stimulate in some families at least an earnest search after something better than they have yet found in their desultory and aimless conversational habits. Surely there should be no home in which amid all the light talk that flies from busy tongues time is not found every day to say at least one word that shall be instructive, suggestive, elevating or in some way helpful.

The home evenings present another field rich with possibilities of lasting influence and holy impression. It is one of the misfortunes of our times that the home is being so robbed of its evenings by business, by pleasure and by society. Some men never spend an evening at home in all the year. Some women do little better. Is it any wonder that in such cases heaven's benediction does not seem to fall upon the household? The days are so full of occupation for most of us, from early morning till nightfall, that whatever real home life we make we must make in the evenings. "To the evening, and especially the winter's evening, belong mainly the influences of domestic life. Its few short hours are all the uninterrupted time we have at our disposal to know our own or be known of them. The impression that home leaves upon the child comes largely from its evenings. The visions which memory delights in conjuring up are the old scenes about the evening fire or the evening lamp."

When we think of the importance of the evenings at home it certainly seems worth while to plan to save as many as possible of them from outside demands for the sacred work within. It were better that we should neglect some social attraction, or miss some political meeting, or be absent from some lodge or society, than that we should neglect the culture of our own homes and let our children slip away from us forever. To allow a boy to spend his evenings on the streets is almost inevitably to indenture him to a life of sin, ending in ruin. The school of the street trains him with amazing rapidity for all manner of crimes. The father who permits his son to go out nightly from the home door amid these unholy influences must not be surprised to learn in a very little time that his boy has learned to smoke, to swear, to drink, to gamble, and that his soul has already been debauched.

But how can we keep our boys off the streets at

night? Can we do it if we ourselves hasten away
from home every evening as soon as we snatch a
hurried supper? If parents would save their boys
they must make a home life for the evenings so
pleasant, so attractive, so charming that they will
not want to leave it for any coarse or glaring fascina-
tions outside. How can this be done? It can be
done if the parents set themselves to do it. There
may be a season of romping if the children are young
— a children's hour devoted to such play as they
will enjoy. There may be pleasant games to pass
away a portion of the evening. There may be the
reading aloud of some racy and interesting book by
one member of the family while the others carry on
the light forms of work which occupy their hands
and eyes, but leave their ears open to hear. There
may be music for a time and bright, cheerful conver-
sation, closing with a prayer and a good-night.

No instruction is needed to teach any intelligent
parent how to give to the evenings at home a charm
which shall make their influence all-potent. It is
necessary only that parents shall set about doing
that which their own hearts tell them so plainly ought
to be done. Of course it will take time. Something
must be left out of life if this is to be done. But is
there anything else in all the round of life's calls, and
even its seeming duties, that might not well be left
out for the sake of anchoring our children to their
homes? Is there anything else that it would be so
fatal and terrible to leave out as to leave our children

out to perish in the ruin of the streets, while we are at lodges and operas and parties, or even at church meetings?

In considering the influences in the home life that leave deep and permanent impressions on character, thought must be given to the books and papers that are read. The invention of the art of printing marked a new era in the world's history. On the printed pages that fly everywhere like the leaves of autumn, drifting to our doors and swept into our innermost chambers, are borne to us the golden thoughts of the best and wisest men and women of all ages. The blessings that the printing press scatters are infinite and rich beyond all estimate. But the same types that to-day give us pure and holy thoughts, words of truth and of life, to-morrow give us veiled suggestions of evil, words of honeyed sweetness, but in which deadly poison is concealed. It is related that one of the soldiers of Cyrus found a casket which was reported to be full of valuable treasures. It was opened, and out of it came a poisonous atmosphere which caused a terrible plague in the army. Many a book that is bound in bright colors has stored within those covers the most deadly moral influences. To open it in a pure home, among young and tender lives, is to let loose evils that never can be gathered back and locked up again.

The printing press puts into the hands of parents a means of good which they may use to the greatest advantage in the culture of their home life and in the shaping of the lives of their household. But they must keep a most diligent watch over the pages that they introduce. They should know the character of every book and paper that comes within their doors, and should resolutely exclude everything that would defile. Then, while they exclude everything whose influence would be for evil, if they are wise they will bring into their home as much as possible of pure, elevating and refining literature. Every beautiful thought that enters a child's mind adds to the strength and loveliness of the character in after days. The educating influence of the best books and papers is incalculable, and no parent can afford to lose it in the training of his family.

Something should be said about home pleasures and amusements. It is a great misfortune if parents suffer themselves to lose the youthful spring and elasticity out of their lives, and to grow away from the spirit of childhood. They should never become old in heart. It was Swedenborg who wrote of heaven that there the oldest angels are the youngest. There is something very striking in the thought. In that blessed Home the members of the family grow always toward youth. Instead of acquiring the marks of age, of care, of exhaustion, they become every day fresher, fairer, fuller of the exuberance of life. It ought to be so in every true earthly home. We cannot stop the years from rolling on, nor can we keep back the gray hairs and the wrinkles and the lines of weariness. These bodies will grow old in spite of us.

But there is no reason why our spirits should not be always young. We ought to keep a child's heart beating in our breast until God calls us up higher. We ought to grow always toward youth. The oldest people in the home ought to be the youngest. If we do grow old it will be bad for our households. There are some homes where the children can scarcely smile without being frowned upon. They are expected to be as grave as if they were fifty and carrying all the burdens of the world upon their shoulders. All the joyousness of their nature is repressed. They are taught to be prim and stiff in their manners. They are continually impressed with the thought that it is a sinful waste of time to play and that it is displeasing to God to have fun and frolic. Some one says: "A great many homes are like the frame of a harp that stands without strings. In form and outline they suggest music, but no melody rises from the empty spaces; and thus it happens that home is unattractive, dreary and dull." There are homes which this picture describes, but they are not the homes that are most like heaven, nor the homes out of which come the truest and noblest lives.

God wants us to fill our homes with happiness. He made childhood joyous, full of life, bubbling over with laughter, playful, bright and sunny. It is a crime to repress the mirth and the gladness and to try to make children grave and stately. Life's burdens will come soon enough to lie upon their shoulders. Life will soon enough bring care and anxiety and hardship and a weight of responsibility. We should let them be young and free from care just as long as possible. We should put into their childhood days just as much sunshine and gladness, just as much cheerful pleasure, as possible. Besides, the way also to make them strong and noble in character when they grow up to manhood and womanhood is to make their childhood and youth bright and happy. If you want to produce a vigorous, healthy plant, you will not bring it up in a dark room; you will give it all the sunshine it will take. Human lives will never grow into their best in gloom. Pour the sunshine about them in youth; let them be happy; encourage all innocent joy; provide pleasant games for them; romp and play with them; be a child again among them. Then God's blessing will come upon your home, and your children will grow up sunny-hearted, gentle, affectionate, joyous themselves and joy-bearers to the world.

When MacMahon returned victorious from the battle of Magenta all Paris came out to welcome him. Many were the honors heaped upon the brave, bronzed soldier. As he was passing in triumph through the streets and boulevards a little child ran out toward him with a bunch of flowers in her hand. He stooped down and lifted her up before him, and she stood there, her arms twining about his neck, as he rode on. This simple exhibition of gentleness toward a little child pleased the people more, and seemed a more beautiful act in their eyes for the moment, than all the memory of his heroic deeds on the battlefield. Men are greatest and best, not when they are wrestling with the world, not when they are putting forth the startling qualities of power, not when they are playing the hero in great contests, but when they are exhibiting most of the spirit of a little child. No parent therefore should ever be ashamed to romp and play with his children. Perhaps he is nearer to God then than when doing what he deems his grandest work in the world. Perhaps the angels applaud more then than when he is performing deeds that bring him praise or fame; and it is better to have fame among the angels than in a dozen worlds.

The young must have amusements. The only question is, What shall be the character of the amusements? Shall they be pure, healthful, refining, elevating? or shall they be degrading in their influence? The parents must answer these questions, and the best way to answer them is to provide in their own home such amusements as they deem proper. If the home is dull and cheerless, it must not.be considered an indication of extraordinary depravity that the children and young people seek pleasure elsewhere. It is as natural as that bees hived in a stubble-field should want to fly over the fence to gather honey from the clover field adjoining. If there is clover at home they will not care to fly abroad. Wise parents will provide amusements for their children, and they will provide them at home, and thus counteract the solicitations of worldly pleasure outside.

There is a great variety of suitable home amusements. One is music. Music is not a mere amusement only, but one that combines rich instruction and lasting influence for good with the purest enjoyment. It is scarcely possible to conceive of any pleasure that surpasses an evening of song in the parlor when the whole family unite in it, perhaps with other friends, one at the piano or organ and the others grouped about, male and female voices blending, now in the pleasant ballad or glee, now in the sacred anthem or hymn. The songs of childhood sung thus into the heart are never forgotten. Their memories live under all the accumulations of busy years, like the sweet flowers that bloom all the winter beneath the heavy snowdrifts. They are remembered in old age when nearly all else is forgotten, and ofttimes sing themselves over again in the heart with voice sweet as an angel's when no other music has power to charm. They neglect one of the richest sources of pleasure and blessing who do not cultivate singing in their homes.

Then there are many games which bring great enjoyment. Chess is delightful to those who have patience and skill to master it, but it requires close thought. There is much enjoyment in the old-fashioned game of checkers. There are many games with various kinds of historical cards, and cards of authors or of birds and animals, which combine exciting pleasure with some instruction. There is scarcely any limit to the number of innocent games from which to make selection for evening amusements. Charades furnish genuine enjoyment. Reading clubs may be so conducted as to yield both pleasure and instruction.

It needs only a heart in full sympathy with youthful feelings, a little skill in arranging and preparing these pleasures, a small expense in furnishing the simple games and other requisites, and interest enough in the matter to devote a little time and pains to it. There is no parent of ordinary intelligence who may not make his home life so bright and sunny that no one will ever care to go outside to seek amusement amid the senseless frivolities or the debasing pleasures that the world offers. Homes that are made thus in all these ways so bright and happy acquire a resistless power over those who live within their doors, which will hold them under its subtle influence wherever they go in all their after years.

There is one experience that comes sooner or later in the life of every home — the experience of sorrow. There may be years of unbroken gladness, but in the end grief is sure to come. The stream that has flowed so long with merry ripple through the green fields and amid the flowers in the bright sunshine, sweeps into the deep shadows, plunges into the dark, sunless gorge, or is hurled over the waterfall. We press our children to our bosom to-day, and love builds up a thousand brilliant hopes for them in our hearts; then to-morrow death comes and they lie silent and still amid the flowers. Or we watch over them and see them grow up into nobleness and beauty, when, just as our dreams and hopes seem about to be realized, the fatal touch is upon them and they are taken away.

There is no need to describe this experience, memory needs no reminder in such cases. The most helpful thing that can be done in these pages is to point out a few of the comforts which should come to every Christian home in such hours.

There is great comfort in the thought that what has befallen us is God's will. Long ago this was the rock on which a godly man leaned when death had come suddenly and taken all: "The Lord gave, and the Lord hath taken away." When we know that God is truly our Father and that his love is eternal and unchangeable, this confidence should give us great peace even in the sorest bereavement.

Another of the great comforts when a little child is taken away is the truth of the immortal life. In the autumn days the birds leave our chill northern clime and we hear their songs no more; but the birds are not dead. In the warmer clime of the far South they live, and amid flowers and fragrant foliage and luscious fruits they continue to sing as joyously as they sang with us in the happiest summer day. So our children leave us, and we miss their sweet faces and prattling voices; but they have only gone to the summer-land of heaven. There in the midst of the glory of the Lord they dwell, shedding their tender grace on other hearts. We all believe this, but most of us believe it in such a way as to get but little comfort from it. The bringing into our hearts of the truth of immortality would take away all bitterness from our sorrow when our little ones leave us.

One of the chief elements of the sorrow when children or young persons die is the sore disappointment. Careers of great usefulness have been marked out for them, and without even entering upon them they are gone. They seem to have lived in vain, to have died without accomplishing any work in this world. So it appears until we think more deeply of it, and then we see that they have not been in this world in vain, though their stay was so brief. They have not done what we had planned for them to do, but they have accomplished the part in God's great plan which he had marked out for them.

Here is a little babe; it lies now in the coffin with a face beautiful as an angel's smile. It lived but a few days or a few months. It merely opened its eyes upon the earth, and then, as if too pure for this world of sin, closed them again and went back to God. Did you say that it lived in vain, that it performed no work? Do you know how many blessings it brought down from heaven to that home when it came like a messenger from the fragrant garden of God, shook its robes and then fled away again? It only crept into the mother's bosom for a brief season and was gone, but ever afterwards her heart will be warmer, her life richer and deeper and her spirit gentler and sweeter. No one can tell what holy work a babe performs that stays only an hour in this world. It does not live in vain. It leaves touches of beauty on other souls which never shall fade out. It may accomplish more in that one short hour, leave greater blessings behind, than do others who live long full years. It may change the eternal destiny of one or more souls. Many a child dying leads an unsaved parent to the sacred feet of Christ. Certain it is that no true parent is ever just the same in character after clasping his own child in his arms. To have felt the warmth and thrill of a new love even for a few moments, though the object loved be withdrawn, leaves a permanent result in the life.

Or perhaps the child lives to be ten or twelve years old. She is the light and joy of the home. Great promises begin to bud and blossom out in her life. Then she dies. As the parents bend over her and kiss her pale, cold lips, they mourn over the crushed hopes that lie there, like buds opening only to be killed by the frost. In imagination they have seen her standing forth in all the splendor of queenly womanhood, crowned with honor, beauty and love. But she has died without realizing these hopes. She has fallen just on the threshold of life. Yet who will say that she did no work in those brief, bright years? She has been a blessing in her home all the time, drawing out the love of tender hearts, scattering influences of joy and purity. Now she is gone, but the work she has done in the home hearts and lives remains and never can be taken away.

THE HOME LIFE

God takes away your children, and in faith you surrender them to him to see them no more in this world; but you cannot give back all that they have brought to you. In your heart new springs of love were opened by their coming; and you cannot give these back. Death cannot take out of your life the new experiences which you had in pressing them to your heart or in loving and caring for them through the sunny years. You are better, stronger, richer in your nature, more a man or a woman, because you have held in your arms and have nurtured your own child. These new outreachings of your life never can be taken from you. Like new branches of a tree they will remain ever after part of yourself. Though the loved ones are removed, the results of their coming to you and staying with you, the influences, the impressions made, the qualities, the new growths in your life, will never depart. They are your permanent possessions forever. Tennyson puts this truth in happy phrase:

> God gives us love; something to love
> He lends us; but when love is grown
> To ripeness, that on which it throve
> Falls off; and love is left alone.

Thus, while the influences of a child's life remain, its death also brings new blessings to the home. It softens all hearts. Rudeness grows gentle under the influence of sorrow. It brings the parents closer together. Many an incipient estrangement is healed at the coffin of a dead child. It is like a new marriage.

There come to many homes other sorrows besides the sorrows of bereavement. There are griefs sorer than those caused by death. There are sorrows over the living who are in peril or who are wandering away, sometimes over those who have fallen. There are wives weeping in secret over trials of which they can speak to none but God. There are parents with sadder disappointments than if they stood by the coffins of their early dead. Sin and shame cause bitterer tears than death. There are homes from which the shadow never lifts, out of which the brightness seems forever to have gone. There are home hearts from which the music has fled, and which are like harps with their strings all broken. Yet even for these there is comfort if they are resting in God's bosom. The divine love can bring blessing out of every possible trial. No life that clings by faith to Christ can be destroyed.

In a lovely Swiss valley there is a cascade which is caught by the swift winds as it pours over the edge of the rock, and scattered so that the falling stream is lost for the time, and only a wreath of whirling spray is seen in the air. But farther down the valley the stream gathers itself back again and pours along in full current in quiet peace, as if it had never been so rudely smitten by the wind. Even the blast that scatters it for the time, and seems to destroy it altogether, really makes it all the lovelier as it whirls its crystal drops into the air. At no other point in all its course is the Staubbach so beautiful.

There are Christian lives that seem to be utterly destroyed by trial, but beyond the sorrow they move on again in calmer, fuller strength, not destroyed, not a particle of their real life wasted. And in the trial itself, through the grace of Christ, their character shines out in richer luster and rarer splendor than ever in the days when their hearts were fullest of joy and gladness.

> "The night is mother of the day,
> The winter of the spring;
> And ever upon old decay
> The greenest mosses cling.
> Behind the cloud the starlight lurks;
> Through showers the sunbeams fall;
> For God, who loveth all his works,
> Hath left his hope with all."

So the life of the true home flows on, sometimes in the bright sunshine, sometimes in the deep shadow; yet whether in sunshine or in shadow it brings blessing. It shelters us in the day of storm. Its friendships remain true and loyal when adversity falls and other friendships are broken. It lays holy hands of benediction upon our heads as we go out to meet life's struggles and duties. Its sacred influences keep us from many a sin. Its memories are our richest inheritance. Its inspirations are the secret strength of our lives in days of toil and care. Then it teaches us to look toward heaven as the great home in which all our hearts' hopes and dreams shall be realized, and where the broken ties of earth shall be reunited.

VIII

FORBEARING ONE ANOTHER

AMONG all Christian duties there are few that touch life at more points than the duty of mutual forbearance, and there are few that, in the observance or the breach, have more to do with the happiness or the unhappiness of life. We cannot live our lives solitarily. We are made to be social beings. It is in our intercourse with others that we find our sweetest pleasures and our purest earthly joys. Yet close by these springs of happiness are other fountains that do not yield sweetness. There often are briers on the branches from which we gather the most luscious fruits. Were human nature perfect, there could be nothing but most tender pleasure in the mutual comminglings of life. But we are all imperfect and full of infirmities. There are qualities in each one of us that are not beautiful — many that are annoying to others. Self rules in greater or less measure in the best of us. In our busy and excited lives we are continually liable to jostle against each other. Our individual interests conflict, or seem to conflict. The things we do in the earnest pressing of our own business and our own plans and efforts seem at times to interfere with the interests of others. In the heat of emulation and the warmth of self-interest we are apt to do things which injure others.

Then, in our closer personal contact, in society and in business relations, we are constantly liable to give pain or offense. We sometimes speak quickly and give expression to thoughtless words which fall like sparks on other inflammable tempers. Even our nearest and truest friends do things that grieve us. Close commingling of imperfect lives always has its manifold little injustices, wrongs, oppressions, slights and grievances.

Then we do not always see each other in clear and honest light. We are prone to have a bias toward self, and often misconstrue the bearing, words or acts of others. Many of us, too, are given to little petulances and expressions of ill-humor or bad temper which greatly lessen the probabilities of unbroken fellowship.

Thus it comes about that no Christian grace is likely to be called into play more frequently than that of mutual forbearance. Without it there can really exist no close and lasting friendly relations in a society composed of imperfect beings. Even the most tender intimacies and the holiest associations require the constant exercise of patience. If we resent every apparent injustice, demand the righting of every little wrong, and insist upon chafing and uttering our feelings at every infinitesimal grievance, and if all the other parties in the circle claim the same privilege, what miserable beings we shall all be, and how wretched life will become!

But there is a more excellent way. The spirit of love inculcated in the New Testament will, if permitted to reign in each heart and life, produce fellowship without a jar or break.

We need to guard first of all against a critical spirit. It is very easy to find fault with people. It is possible, even with ordinary glasses, to see many things in one another that are not what they ought to be. Then some people carry microscopes fine enough to reveal a million animalculæ in a drop of water, and with these they can find countless blemishes in the character and conduct even of the most saintly dwellers on the earth. There are some who are always watching for slights and grievances. They are suspicious of the motives and intentions of others. They are always imagining offenses, even where none were most remotely intended. This habit is directly at variance with the law of love, which thinketh no evil.

We turn to the Pattern. Does Christ look upon us sharply, critically, suspiciously? He sees every infirmity in us, but it is as though he did not see it. His love overlooks it. He throws a veil over our faults. He continues to pour his own love upon us in spite of all our blemishes and our ill treatment of him. The law of Christian forbearance requires the same in us. We must not keep our selfish suspicions ever on the watch-tower or at the windows, looking out for neglects, discourtesies, wrongs, or grievances of any kind. We had better be blind, not perceiving at all the seeming rudeness or insult. It is well not to hear all that is said, or, if hear we must, to be as though we heard not.

Many bitter quarrels have grown out of an imagined slight, many out of an utter misconception, or perchance from the misrepresentation of some wretched gossipmonger. Had a few moments been given to ascertain the truth, there had never been any occasion for ill-feeling.

We should seek to know the motive also which prompts the apparent grievance. In many cases the cause of our grievance is utterly unintentional, chargeable to nothing worse than thoughtlessness — possibly meant even for kindness. It is never fair to judge men by every word they speak or everything they do in the excitement and amid the irritations of busy daily life. Many a gruff man carries a good heart and a sincere friendship under his coarse manner. The best does not always come to the surface. We should never, therefore, hastily imagine evil intention in others. Nor should we allow ourselves to be easily persuaded that our companions or friends meant to treat us unkindly. A disposition to look favorably upon the conduct of our fellow men is a wonderful absorber of the frictions of life.

Then there are always cases of real injustice. There are rudenesses and wrongs which we cannot regard as merely imaginary or as misconceptions. They proceed from bad temper or from jealousy or malice, and are very hard to bear. Kindness is repaid with unkindness. We find impatience and petulance in our best friends. There are countless things every day in our associations with others which tend to vex or irritate us.

Here is room for the fullest exercise of that divinely beautiful charity which covers a multitude of sins in others. We seek to make every possible excuse for the neglect or rudeness or wrong. Perhaps our friend is carrying some perplexing care or some great burden to-day. Something may be going wrong in his business or at his home. Or it may be his unstrung nerves that make him so thoughtless and inconsiderate. Or his bad health may be the cause. A large-hearted spirit will always seek to find some palliation at least for the apparent wrong.

Another step in the school of forbearance is the lesson of keeping silent under provocation. One person alone can never make a quarrel: it takes two. A homely counsel to a newly married couple was that they should never both be angry at the same time — that one should always remain calm and tranquil. There is a still diviner counsel which speaks of the soft answer which turneth away wrath. If we cannot have the soft answer always ready, we can at least learn not to answer at all. Our Lord met nearly all the insults he received with patient uncomplaining silence. He was like a lamb dumb before the shearer. All the keen insults of the cruel throng wrung from him no word of resentment, no look of impatience. As the fragrant perfume but gives forth added sweetness when crushed, so cruelty, wrong and pain only made him be gentler and the love that always distinguished him be sweeter.

It is a majestic power, this power of keeping silent. Great is the conqueror who leads armies to victories. Mighty is the strength that captures a city. But he is greater who can rule his own spirit. There are men who can command armies, but cannot command themselves. There are men who by their burning words can sway vast multitudes who cannot keep silence under provocation or wrong. The highest mark of nobility is self-control. It is more kingly than regal crown and purple robe.

> "Not in the clamor of the crowded street,
>   Not in the shouts and plaudits of the throng,
>   But in ourselves, are triumph and defeat."

There are times when silence is golden, when words mean defeat, and when victory can be gained only by answering not a word. Many of the painful quarrels and much of the bitterness of what we call so often "incompatibility of temper" would never be known if we would learn to keep silence when others wrong us. We may choke back the angry word that flies to our lips. The insult unanswered will recoil upon itself and be its own destruction.

There is also a wonderful opportunity here for the play of good nature. There are some people whose abounding humor always comes to their relief when they observe the gathering of a storm, and they will have a little story ready, or will suddenly turn the conversation entirely away from the inflammable subject, or will make some bright or playful remark that will cause the whole trouble to blow off in a hearty laugh. It would not seem impossible for all to learn to bear insults or grievances in some of these ways, either in silence — not sullen, thunder-charged, but loving silence — or by returning the soft answer which will quench the flame of anger, or by that wise tact which drives out the petulant humor by the explosive power of a new emotion.

There are at least two motives which should be sufficient to lead us to cultivate this grace of forbearance. One is that no insult can do us harm unless we allow it to irritate us. If we endure even the sorest words as Jesus endured his wrongs and revilings, they will not leave one trace of injury upon us. They can harm us only when we allow ourselves to become impatient or angry. We can get the victory over them, utterly disarm them of power to do us injury, by holding ourselves superior to them. The feeling of resentment will change to pity when we remember that not he who is wronged, but he who does the wrong, is the one who suffers. Every injustice or grievance reacts and leaves a stain and a wound. All the cruelties and persecutions that human hate could inflict would not leave one trace of real harm upon us, but every feeling of resentment admitted into our hearts, every angry word uttered, will leave a stain. Forbearance thus becomes a perfect shield which protects us from all the cruelties and wrongs of life.

The other motive is drawn from our relation to God. We sin against him continually, and his mercy never fails. His love bears with all our neglect, forgetfulness, ingratitude and disobedience, and never grows impatient with us. We live only by his forbearance. The wrongs he endures from us are infinite in comparison with the trivial grievances we must endure from our fellow men. When we think of this, can we grow impatient of the little irritations of daily fellowship? We are taught to pray every day, "Forgive us our debts as we forgive our debtors." How can we pray this petition sincerely and continue to be exacting, resentful, revengeful, or even to be greatly pained by the unkind treatment of others?

God is slow to see our sins or to write them down against us. He delights in mercy. We are to repeat in our lives as his children something at least of his patience. The song of forgiveness and forbearance which he sings into our hearts we are to echo forth again.

IX

ABOUT TEMPER

BAD temper is such a disfigurement of character, and, besides, works such harm to oneself and to one's neighbors, that no one should spare any pains or cost to have it cured. The ideal Christian life is one of unbroken kindliness. It is dominated by love — the love whose portrait is drawn for us in the immortal thirteenth of First Corinthians. It suffereth long and is kind. It envieth not. It vaunteth not itself, is not puffed up, doth not behave itself unseemly, seeketh not its own, is not provoked, taketh not account of evil; beareth all things, believeth all things, hopeth all things, endureth all things. That is the picture; then we have but to turn to the gospel pages to find the story of a Life in which all this was realized. Jesus never lost his temper. He lived among people who tried him at every point — some by their dullness, others by their bitter enmity and persecution — but he never failed in sweetness of disposition, in long-suffering patience, in self-denying love. Like the flowers which give out their perfume only when crushed, like the odoriferous wood which bathes with fragrance the ax which hews it, the life of Christ yielded only the tenderer, sweeter love to the rough impact of men's rudeness and wrong. That is the pattern on which we should strive to fashion our life and our character. Every outbreak of violent temper, every shade of ugliness in disposition, mars the radiant loveliness of the picture we are seeking to have fashioned in our souls. Whatever is not loving is unlovely.

There is another phase: bad-tempered people are continually hurting others, ofttimes their best and truest friends. Some people are sulky, and one person's sulkiness casts a chilling shadow over a whole household; others are so sensitive, ever watching for slights and offended by the merest trifles, that even their nearest friends have no freedom of intercourse with them; others are despotic, and will brook no kindly suggestion nor listen to any expression of opinion; others are so quarrelsome that even the meekest and gentlest person cannot live peaceably with them. Whatever may be the special characteristic of the bad temper, it makes only pain and humiliation for the person's friends.

A bad temper usually implies a sharp tongue. Sometimes, indeed, it makes one morose and glum. A brother and a sister living together are said often to have passed months without speaking to each other, though eating at the same table and sleeping under the same roof. A man recently died who for twelve years, it was said, had never spoken to his wife, though they continued to dwell together, and three times daily sat down together at the same table. Bad temper sometimes runs to proud silence. Such silence is not golden. Generally, however, a bad-tempered person has an unbridled tongue and speaks out his hateful feelings; and there is no limit to the pain and the harm which angry and ugly words can produce in gentle hearts.

It would be easy to extend this portrayal of the evils of bad temper, but it will be more profitable to inquire how a bad-tempered person may become good-tempered. There is no doubt that this happy change is possible in any case. There is no temper so obdurately bad that it cannot be trained into sweetness. The grace of God can take the most unlovely life and transform it into the image of Christ. As in all moral changes, however, grace does not work independently of human volition and exertion: God always works helpfully with those who strive to reach Christlikeness. We must resist the Devil, or he will not flee from us. We must struggle to obtain the victory over our own evil habits and dispositions, although it is only through Christ that we can be conquerors; he will not make us conquerors unless we enter the battle. We have a share, and a large and necessary share, in the culture of our own character. The bad-tempered man will never become good-tempered until he deliberately sets for · himself the task and enters resolutely and persistently upon its accomplishment. The transformation will never come of itself even in a Christian. People do not grow out of ugly temper into sweet refinement as a peach ripens from sourness into lusciousness.

Then the thing to be accomplished is not the destroying of the temper; temper is a good quality in its place. The task is not destruction, but control. A man is very weak who has a strong temper without the power of self-control; likewise is he weak who has a weak temper. The truly strong man is he who is strong in the element of temper — that is, has strong passions and feelings capable of great anger, and then has perfect self-control. When Moses failed and broke down in temper, self-control, he was not the man to lead the people into the Promised Land; therefore God at once prepared to relieve him. The task to be set before us in self-discipline is the gaining of complete mastery over every feeling and emotion, so as to be able to restrain every impulse to speak or to act unadvisedly.

Then there is need of a higher standard of character in this regard than many people seem to set for themselves. We never rise higher than our ideals; the perfect beauty of Christ should ever be visioned in our hearts as that which we would attain for ourselves. The honor of our Master's name should impel us to strive ever toward Christlikeness in spirit and in disposition. We represent Christ in this world; people cannot see him, and they must look at us to see a little of what he is like. Whatever

great work we may do for Christ, if we fail to live
out his life of patience and forbearance, we fail in
an essential part of our duty as Christians. "The
servant of the Lord must be . . . gentle."

Nor can we be greatly useful in our personal life
while our daily conduct is stained by frequent out-
bursts of anger and other exhibitions of temper.
In the old fable the spider goes about doing mischief
wherever it creeps, while the bee by its wax and its
honey makes "sweetness and light" wherever it
flies. We had better be bees than be spiders, living
to turn darkness into light and to put a little more
sweetness into the life of all who know us. But only
as our own lives shine in the brightness of holy affec-
tionateness and our hearts and lips distill the sweetness
of patience and gentleness can we fulfill our mission
in this world as Christ's true messengers to men.

In striving to overcome our impatience with
others it will help us to remember that we and they
have the common heritage of a sinful nature. The
thing in them which irritates us is, no doubt, balanced
by something in us which looks just as unlovely in
their eyes and just as sorely tries their forbearance
toward us. Whittier wisely says:

> Search thine own heart. What paineth thee
> In others, in thyself may be.
> All dust is frail, all flesh is weak:
> Be thou the true man thou dost seek.

Very likely, if we think our neighbors hard to
live peaceably with, they think about the same of

us; and who shall tell in whom lies the greater
degree of fault? Certain it is that a really good-
tempered person can rarely ever be drawn into a
quarrel with anyone. He is resolutely determined
that he will not be a partner in any unseemly strife;
he would rather suffer wrongfully than offer any re-
taliation; he has learned to bear and to forbear.
Then by his gentle tact he is able to conciliate any
who are angry.

A fable relates that in the depth of a forest there
lived two foxes. One of them said to the other
one day in the politest of fox-language, "Let's quar-
rel." "Very well," said the other; "but how shall
we set about it?" They tried all sorts of ways, but
in vain, for both would give way. At last one
brought two stones. "There!" said he. "Now you
say they are yours and I'll say they are mine, and
we will quarrel and fight and scratch. Now I'll
begin. Those stones are mine." "All right!"
answered the other fox; "you are welcome to them."
"But we shall never quarrel at this rate," replied
the first. "No, indeed, you old simpleton! Don't
you know it takes two to make a quarrel?" So the
foxes gave up trying to quarrel, and never played
again at this silly game.

The fable has its lesson for other creatures besides
foxes. As far as in us lies, Paul tells us, we should
live peaceably with all men. A wise man says,
"Every man takes care that his neighbors shall not
cheat him, but a day comes when he begins to care

that he does not cheat his neighbors. Then all goes
well. He has changed his market-cart into a chariot
of the sun." So long as a man sees only the quarrel-
some temper of his neighbor he is not far toward
saintliness; but when he has learned to watch and
to try to control his own temper and to weep over
his own infirmities, he is on the way to God, and will
soon be conqueror over his own weakness.

Life is too short to spend even one day of it in
bickering and strife; love is too sacred to be for-
ever lacerated and torn by the ugly briers of sharp
temper. Surely we ought to learn to be patient with
others, since God has to show every day such infinite
patience toward us. Is not the very essence of true
love the spirit that is not easily provoked, that
beareth all things? Can we not, then, train our life
to sweeter gentleness? Can we not learn to be touched
even a little roughly without resenting it? Can we
not bear little injuries and apparent injustices with-
out flying into an unseemly rage? Can we not have
in us something of the mind of Christ which will
enable us, like him, to endure all wrong and injury
and give back no word or look of bitterness? The
way over which we and our friend walk together is
too short to be spent in wrangling.

THE BLESSING OF QUIETNESS

Drop Thy still dews of quietness
    Till all our strivings cease;
Take from our souls the strain and stress,
And let our ordered lives confess
    The beauty of thy peace.

WHITTIER.

QUIETNESS, like mercy, is twice blessed: it blesseth him that is quiet, and it blesseth the man's friends and neighbors. Talk is good in its way. "There is a time to speak," but there is also "a time to be silent," and in silence many of life's sweetest benedictions come.

An Italian proverb says, "He that speaks doth sow; he that holds his peace doth reap." We all know the other saying which rates speech as silver and silence as gold. There are in the Scriptures, too, many strong persuasives to quietness and many exhortations against noise. It was prophesied of the Christ: "He shall not cry, nor lift up, nor cause his voice to be heard in the street." As we read the Gospels we see that our Lord's whole life was a fulfillment of this ancient prophecy. He made

[161]

no noise in the world. He did his work without excitement, without parade, without confusion. He wrought as the light works — silently, yet pervasively and with resistless energy.

Quietness is urged, too, on Christ's followers. "Study to be quiet," writes an apostle. "Busybodies" the same apostle exhorts that "with quietness they work." Prayers are to be made for rulers "that we may lead a quiet and peaceable life." Another apostle, writing to Christian women, speaks of their true adornment as being "the ornament of a meek and quiet spirit, which is in the sight of God of great price." Solomon rates quietness in a home far above the best of luxuries:

> Better is a dry morsel and quietness therewith,
> Than an house full of feasting with strife.

A prophet declares the secret of power in these words: "In quietness and confidence shall be your strength"; and likewise says, "The work of righteousness shall be peace, and the effect of righteousness quietness and assurance for ever." It is set down also as one of the blessings of God's people that they shall dwell in "quiet resting-places."

These are but a few of very many scriptural words concerning quietness, but they are enough to indicate several lessons that we may profitably consider.

We should be quiet toward God. The expression "Rest in the Lord," in one of the Psalms, is in the margin "Be silent to the Lord." We are not to speak back to God when he speaks to us. We are not to reason with him or dispute with him, but are to bow in silent and loving acquiescence before him: "Be still, and know that I am God." It is in those providences which cut sorely into our lives and require sacrifice and loss on our part that we are specially called to this duty. There is a pathetic illustration of silence to God in the case of Aaron when his sons had offered strange fire, and had died before the Lord for their disobedience and sacrilege. The record says, "And Aaron held his peace." He even made no natural human outcry of grief. He accepted the terrible penalty as unquestionably just, and bowed in the acquiescence of faith.

This silence to God should be our attitude in all times of trial when God's ways with us are bitter and painful. Why should we complain at anything that our Father may do? We have no right to utter a word of murmuring, for he is our sovereign Lord, and our simple duty is instant, unquestioning submission. Then we have no reason to complain, for we know that all God's dealings with us are in loving wisdom. His will is always best for us, whatever sacrifice or suffering it may cost.

> "Thou layest thy hand on the fluttering heart,
> And sayest, 'Be still!'
> The silence and shadow are only a part
> Of thy sweet will;
> Thy presence is with me, and where thou art
> I fear no ill."

[163]

THE HOME BEAUTIFUL

We should train ourselves to be quiet also toward
men. There are times when we should speak and
when words are mighty and full of blessing. Uni-
versal dumbness would not be a boon to the world.
Among the most beneficent of God's gifts to us is
the power of speech. And we are to use our tongues.
There are some people who are altogether too quiet
in certain directions and toward certain persons.
There is no place where good words are more fitting
than between husband and wife, yet there are hus-
bands and wives who pass weeks and months together
in almost unbroken silence. They will travel long
journeys side by side in the railway-car, and utter
scarcely a word in the whole distance. They will
walk to and from church, and neither will speak.
In the home life they will pass whole days with noth-
ing more in the form of speech between them than
an indifferent remark about the weather, a formal
inquiry and a monosyllabic answer.

"According to Milton, Eve kept silence in Eden
to hear her husband talk," said a gentleman to a
lady, adding in a melancholy tone, "Alas! there
have been no Eves since!" "Because," quickly
retorted the lady, "there have been no husbands
worth listening to." Perhaps the retort was just.
Husbands certainly ought to have something to say
when they come into their homes from the busy world
outside. They are usually genial enough in the
circles of business or politics or literature, and are
able to talk so as to interest others. Ought they

THE BLESSING OF QUIETNESS

not to seek to be as genial in their own homes, especially toward their own wives? Most women, too, are able to talk in general society. Why, then, should a wife fall into such a mood of silence the moment she and her husband are alone? It was Franklin who wisely said, "As we must account for every idle word, so must we for every idle silence." We must not forget that silence may be sadly overdone, especially in homes.

There are other silences that are also to be deplored. People keep in their hearts unspoken the kindly words they might utter — ought to utter — in the ears of the weary, the soul-hungry and the sorrowing about them. The ministry of good words is one of wondrous power, yet many of us are wretched misers with our gold and silver coin of speech. Is any miserliness so mean? Ofttimes we allow hearts to starve close beside us, though in our very hands we have abundance to feed them. One who attends the funeral of any ordinary man and listens to what his neighbors have to say about him as they stand by his coffin will hear enough kind words spoken to have brightened whole years of his life. But how was it when the man was living, toiling and struggling among these very people? Ah! they were not so faithful then with their grateful, appreciative words. They were too quiet toward him then. Silence was overdone.

Quietness is carried too far when it makes us disloyal to the hearts that crave our words of love and sympathy. But there is a quietness toward others which all should cultivate. There are many words spoken which ought never to pass the door of the lips. There are people who seem to exercise no restraint whatever on their speech. They allow every passing thought or feeling to take form in words. They never think what the effect of their words will be — how they will fly like arrows shot by some careless marksman and will pierce hearts they were never meant to hurt. Thus friendships are broken and injuries are inflicted which can never be repaired. Careless words are forever making grief and sorrow in tender spirits. We pity the dumb whom sometimes we meet. Dumbness is more blessed by far than speech if all we can do with our marvelous gift is to utter bitter, angry, abusive or sharp, cutting words.

Another kind of common talk that had better be repressed into complete silence is the miserable gossip which forms so large a part — let us confess it and deplore it — of ordinary parlor conversation. Few appreciative and kindly things are spoken of absent ones, but there is no end to criticism, snarling and backbiting. The most unsavory bits of scandal are served with relish, and no character is proof against the virulence and maliciousness of the tongues that chatter on as innocently and glibly as if they were telling sweet stories of good. It certainly would be infinitely better if all this kind of speech were reduced to utter silence. It were better that the ritual of fashion prescribed some sort of a dumb pantomime for social calls, receptions and tête-à-têtes in place of any conversation whatsoever if there is nothing to be talked about but the faults and foibles and the characters and doings of absent people. Will not some new Peter the Hermit preach a crusade against backbiting? Shall we not have a new annual "week of prayer" to cry to God for the gift of silence when we have nothing good or true or beautiful to say? No victories should be more heroically battled for or more thankfully recorded than victories of silence when we are tempted to speak unhallowed words of others.

Silence is better, also, than any words of bickering and strife. There is no surer, better way of preventing quarrels than by the firm restraining of speech. "A soft answer turneth away wrath;" but if we cannot command the "soft answer" when another person is angry, the second-best thing is not to speak at all. "Grievous words stir up anger." Many a long, fierce strife that has produced untold pain and heartburning would never have been anything more than a momentary flash of anger if one of the parties had practiced the holy art of silence.

Some one tells of the following arrangement which worked successfully in preventing family quarrels: "You see, sir," said an old man, speaking of a couple in his neighborhood who lived in perfect harmony, "they had agreed between themselves that whenever he came home a little contrary and out of temper he would wear his hat on the back of his head, and then she never said a word; and if she came in a little cross and crooked, she would throw her shawl over her left shoulder, and he never said a word." So they never quarreled.

He who has learned to be silent spares himself ofttimes from confusion. Many men have owed their reputation for great wisdom quite as much to their silence as to their speech. They have not spoken the many foolish things of the glib talker, and have uttered only few and well-considered words. Says Carlyle, denouncing the rapid verbiage of shallow praters, "Even triviality and imbecility that can sit silent — how respectable are they in comparison!" An English writer gives the story of a groom wedded to a lady of wealth. He was in constant fear of being ridiculed by his wife's guests. A clergyman said to him, "Wear a black coat and hold your tongue." The new husband followed the advice, and soon was considered one of the finest gentlemen in the country. The power of keeping quiet would be worth a great deal to many people whose tongues are forever betraying their ignorance and revealing their true character.

All true culture is toward the control and the restraining of speech. Christian faith gives a quietness which in itself is one of life's holiest benedictions. It gives the quietness of peace — a quietness which the wildest storms cannot disturb, which is a richer possession than all the world's wealth or power.

THE BLESSING OF QUIETNESS

"Study to be quiet." The lesson may be hard to many of us, but it is well worth all the cost of learning. It brings strength and peace to the heart. Speech is good, but ofttimes silence is better. He who has learned to hold his tongue is a greater conqueror than the warrior who subdues an empire. The power to be silent under provocations and wrongs and in the midst of danger and alarms is the power of the noblest, royalest victoriousness.

RELIGION IN THE HOME

WHAT is it that makes a home complete after all that the architect, the builder, the painter, the upholsterer, the furniture-maker and the decorator can do? What is it that comes into the furnished house and makes it a home? This is the question to which answer has been sought in all the former pages of this little book. The duties of the several members of the household have been considered. Suppose they all do their part with the highest fidelity possible in this world; what more is needed to complete the Ideal Christian Home? Is not the answer found in one word — God? If we leave him out our most perfect home will be but like a marble statue, with all the grace and beauty of life, but having neither breath nor heart-throb.

There are many reasons why religion is needed to complete the happiness and blessedness of a home. One is that nothing in this world is full and complete without the benediction of heaven. "The blessing of the Lord, it maketh rich." All that labor and skill and soil and seeds can do for field or garden

will not avail unless heaven give rain and sunshine.
Our very breath is God's gift, moment by moment.
Our daily bread must come day by day from his
hand. All our plans are dependent upon his prosper-
ing favor. Nothing can succeed without his approval
and help. We are taught in the Scriptures to look
to God for his blessing on every undertaking. The
people were to bring the first sheaf of their harvest
and the first ripe clusters from their vineyard to God's
altar, before they had reaped a handful or gathered
a grape for themselves, that his blessing might rest
upon the whole harvest and vintage. They were to
bring their children to God in the very opening of
their life for consecration to him, that his blessing
might rest upon all their years. In the old patri-
archal days, when the tent was set up, if only for a
night, an altar was also erected and sacrifices of
prayer and praise were offered to God.

We need the divine blessing on everything we have
and everything we do. Surely there is no work, no
plan, no undertaking, in all the range of the possible
things we may do in the longest and busiest lifetime,
on which we so much need God's benediction as upon
our home. In nothing else are so many sacred
interests and such momentous responsibilities in-
volved. Nowhere else in life do we meet such diffi-
cult and delicate duties. In nothing else is failure
so disastrous. A business venture may miscarry,
and the consequences will be much chargin and dis-
appointment, some pecuniary loss, some hardship

and suffering; but if one's home is a failure, who can tell what wreck and sorrow may result? If we need the divine blessing on some little work of an hour, how much more do we need it in the setting up of our home, which carries in itself our own happiness and the happiness of the hearts that are dearest to us, and the eternal destinies of souls that shall creep into our bosom and find shelter beneath our roof!

I have read that when the stones were all being carried away, one by one, from an old ruin in Rome, thus destroying one of the grandest relics of antiquity, the ruling pontiff, to preserve it, set up a cross in the midst of it, consecrating it by this act. It was thus made holy, and no one would touch it. The venerable pile was saved in this way from spoliation.

Every home in this world is exposed to a thousand dangers. Enemies seek to destroy it, to desecrate its holy beauty and to carry away its sacred treasures. The very institution itself is assailed by the apostles of infidelity and licentiousness. Countless social influences tend to disintegrate the home, to rob it of its sanctities, to break down its sacred barriers and to sully its purity. Nothing but the cross of Christ will save it. Those who are setting up a home, their hearts full of precious hopes of happiness and blessing, should consecrate it at once by erecting the altar of God in the midst of it. This will throw over it the protecting ægis of divine love.

We need religion in our homes to help us to do each his own part faithfully. Take the parents, for example — whose duties and responsibilities have been considered in a former chapter — into whose hands come tender young lives with infinite possibilities of development. They are to train these immortal souls into beauty and build up in them a noble manhood or womanhood. These lives are so sensitive that the slightest influences will leave imperishable impressions upon them, that a wrong touch may mar them forever. They may have in them the elements of great power or usefulness; God may want them trained to be leaders in the world. For the upbuilding of their character, for the impressions that shall be stamped upon their souls, for their protection from unholy influences, for the molding and shaping of their lives, for the development and training of their powers and for their preparation for life's mission and for eternity, the parents are responsible. Who is sufficient alone for these things? Where is the parent who feels ready in himself to assume all this responsibility — to take an infant child from God's hands to be tended, sheltered, taught, trained and led, and to answer at the end before God's bar for the faithful keeping of his sacred trust? Where is the parent who is prepared to engage to do all this and who wants no help from God? That so many do become fathers and mothers who never ask divine aid and wisdom only proves how thoughtlessly men and women can enter the most solemn mysteries of life, and with how little conception of their responsibility they accept the most momentous duties.

Only the religion of Christ can fit parents for their high and holy responsibility.

We need religion in our homes in the time of sorrow. And where is the home into which sorrow comes not? We can build no walls strong enough or high enough to shut it out. We can gather within our doors no treasures so sacred that sorrow will never lay its hand upon them. Then when sorrow comes where shall we find comfort if not in the religion of Jesus Christ? Shall we find anything in the splendors of architecture, in the beauties of art, in the luxuries of costly furnishing or adorning, to bring calm and comfort to our hearts when one of our household lies in the struggle of death?

But in the home of prayer when trial comes there is help at hand. An unseen presence walks amid the shadows. A voice others hear not whispers peace. A hand others see not ministers consolation. Religion pours light in the darkness. The sorrow is no less bitter, but the stricken hearts are sustained in their pain or loss by the rich consolations of divine love. No home is prepared for the trials which are at some time inevitable which has not its altar standing in the center, whereon the fires burn perpetually.

Every home needs the refuge of religion. We live in a world of danger. Every life that grows up here must grow up amid countless perils. Human souls are delicate and tender. Our dear ones are exposed on every hand. Storms sweep the sea and the wreck goes down, burying noble lives beneath the waves; there is sorrow in homes when the missing ones come not. The battle rages on the bloody field and many a brave soldier falls to rise no more, or to rise scarred, maimed for life; there is grief in the homes where the cruel ball strikes. But there are fiercer storms raging in this world than those upon the sea, and our dear ones are exposed to them. There are more terrific battles on earth than those whose crash makes the mountains shake and which decide the fate of nations, and the tender souls of our households are in the very center of the strife.

When our children go out from us in the morning to the day's duties, or in the evening to the night's scenes and pleasures, we know not to what terrible dangers they will be exposed before we see them again. We mourn for our dead, but if they have died in the arms of Christ they are safe. No danger ever can reach them. They have no more battles to fight. Do we never weep for our living when we remember to what perils they are exposed?

"Lord, we can trust thee for our holy dead;
   They, underneath the shadow of thy tomb,
Have entered into peace; with bended head
   We thank thee for their rest, and for our lightened gloom.

"But, Lord, our living — who on stormy seas
   Of sin and sorrow still are tempest-tossed!
Our dead have reached their haven, but for these —
   Teach us to trust thee, Lord, for these, our loved and lost.

"For these we make our passion-prayer at night;
   For these we cry to thee through the long day."

Yes, our dead in Christ are safe. They are folded away under the shadow of God's wings.

> "What is death, father?"
>   "The rest, my child,
>   When the strife and toil are o'er;
> The angel of God — who, calm and mild,
>   Says we need fight no more;
> Who, driving away the demon band,
>   Bids the din of the battle cease, —
> Takes banner and spear from our trembling hand,
>   And proclaims an eternal peace."

The children that we laid in Christ's arms in infancy, in the sleep we call death, are forever safe. It is our living that are in peril. It is life that is hard and full of danger; it is for our living that we need to be anxious, lest they be defeated in the field, where foes are thick and battles sore.

Where shall we find protection for these tender lives save in the keeping of the almighty Saviour? We cannot shelter them ourselves. We cannot make our home doors strong enough to shield them. We cannot protect them even by love's tenderness or by the influence of beautiful things — of art, of luxury, of music, or by the refinements of the truest and best culture. From amid all these things children's souls are every day stolen away. All history and all experience proves that nothing but the religion of Christ can be a shelter for our loved ones from this world's dangers and temptations.

A friend was telling of a wonderful little flower which he discovered high up on the Rocky Mountains. In a deep fissure among the rocks, one mid-summer day, he found the snow still lying unmelted, and on the surface of the snow he saw a lovely flower. When he looked closely he perceived that it had a long, delicate stem, white as a tuberose, coming up through the deep snow from the soil in a crevice of the rock underneath. The little plant had grown up in spite of all obstacles, its tender stem unharmed by the cold drifts, until it blossomed out in loveliness above the snow. The secret was its root in the rich soil in the cleft of the rock, from which it drew such fulness of life that it rose through all to perfect beauty. Fit picture is that little flower of every tender child-life in this world. Over it are chilling masses of evil and destructive influences, and if it ever grows up into noble and lovely character it must conquer its way by the force of its own inward life, until it stands crowned with beauty, with every obstacle beneath it. This it can do only through the power of the divine grace within. Its root must be homed in the sheltered warmth of piety, in the cleft of the Rock of Ages. Those who grow up in truly Christian homes, imbibing in their souls from infancy the very life of Christ, will be strong to overcome every obstacle and resist every temptation. The influence of godly example, the memories of the home altar, the abiding power of holy teachings and the grace of God descending perpetually upon the young life in answer to believing prayer, give it such inspirations and impulses toward all that is noble and heavenly that it will stand at last crowned with honor and beauty. To make a home godless and prayerless is to send our children out to meet all the world's evil without either the shelter of covenant love to cover them in the storm or the strength of holy principle in their hearts to make them able to endure.

But what is it that makes a home a Christian home? What is home religion? These questions are important enough for most thoughtful consideration. Those who wish to cultivate flowers so as to bring out the richest possible beauty in them study long and diligently the nature of plant life and the many conditions of soil, of temperature, of air and moisture essential to the growth of each particular kind of plant and the development of each variety of flower, and then with scientific exactness produce in each case the right conditions. In our homes we are growing immortal lives. The problem is to bring out in each one the very highest possible development of manly or womanly character. There are certain conditions which are essential to all true growth. If men take such pains to know how to grow flowers which fade in a day, should we not take pains to know how to grow souls which live forever?

What should be the religious atmosphere of a home to make it a true spiritual conservatory?

There must be a home altar. No Christian home life can be complete where the family do not daily gather for worship. All the members may meet in

RELIGION IN THE HOME

God's house on the Sabbath for public service; each one may maintain strict habits of secret devotion; but if there is to be a family religion, a home life blessed and sweetened by the grace of Christ, there must also be a family worship where all assemble to listen devoutly to God's Word and bow reverently in supplication at God's feet.

There are many reasons why such worship should be observed. Shall we take all God's daily benefits from his hand and return to him no thanks? Shall we be dependent continually on his bountiful providence for food, for raiment, for protection, for love and all the tender joys of home, and shall we never ask him for one of these blessings?

Shall we call our home a Christian home, and yet never worship Christ within our doors? Shall we call ourselves God's children, and yet never offer any praise to our Father? Should there not be some difference between a Christian and a heathen home? Should not God's children live differently from the children of this world? What mark is there that distinguishes our home from the home of our godless neighbor if there be no family altar?

There are many things that tend to cause friction in a household. There are daily cares. There are annoyances of a thousand kinds that break in upon the even flow of the family life. None of us are angels, and our intercourse together is ofttimes marred by selfishness or impatience or irritability or querulousness. Sometimes our quick lips speak the harsh word that gives pain to more than one tender heart in the household. We sometimes misunderstand each other, and a shadow hangs between two souls which love each other very truly. There is nothing that will smooth out all the little tangles and set all wrong things right again like the daily worship together. Every burden is there brought and laid off on the great Burden-bearer. Harsh feelings are softened as the admonitions of God's Word fall on the ear. Hearts are drawn closer together as they approach the same throne of heavenly grace and feel the Spirit's power. Impatience vanishes from face and speech while all wait together before God. No bitterness against another member of the family can live through a tender season of household worship; while we plead with God to forgive our sins we cannot but forgive one another. Peace comes to the perplexed soul while bowing at God's feet and feeling the great calm of his own peace brooding over us and lying all about us. We are ashamed of our disquiet and worry when we look up into our Father's face and see how faithfully he loves and cares for us.

Bowing in prayer together in the morning strengthens all the household for life's active duties. Wisdom is sought and obtained for the decisions and plans of the day. Guidance is asked and received. Help is drawn down from the throne of God. The children go out under sheltering wings and are safe in danger, guarded by angels and kept by Christ himself.

Thus reasons multiply why there should be family worship in every home. It is hard to see how any parent who realizes his responsibility can fail to have his household altar. Consider the matter frankly and honestly. You are a Christian man or a Christian woman. Your children look to you for the witness of Christ. What do they think of the absence of family prayer in their home? How does it impress them? Is your testimony before them what it should be? Can your religious life stamp itself on them if you never bow with them in prayer? Are you bringing to bear upon their tender lives all the hallowing influences needed to purify and keep pure the fountains of their hearts? You want their characters to be permeated with the truths of God's Word. Can you hope that this will be so if they are not from childhood accustomed daily to hear these truths in their own homes? It is impossible to estimate the influence of the reading of the Word in a home day after day and year after year. It filters into the hearts of the young. It is absorbed into their souls. It colors all their thoughts. It is wrought into the very fiber of their minds. It imbues them with its own spirit. Its holy teachings become the principles of their lives, which rule their conduct and shape all their actions.

Where every day the Bible is read in a home in the ears of the children, and its lessons simply and prayerfully taught, the effect is incalculable. It was thus that God himself commanded his ancient people to do, to teach the truths of his Word diligently to their children when they sat in the house and when they walked by the way, when they rose up and when they lay down.[1] This was the divine plan for bringing up a family — not a lesson now and then, but the incessant, uninterrupted and continuous teaching of the Holy Scripture in the ears of the children. Such teaching unconsciously assimilates the character to the divine likeness. Can any parents who desire to see their children Christians afford to lose out of the school for their nurture these mighty influences? Even if there were no family prayer, the mere daily reading of the Scriptures year after year continuously would be in itself an inestimable influence for good. But where prayer is added, the household waiting together daily around God's feet while heavenly gifts and favors are tenderly supplicated, who can sum up the total of blessing? What parent can afford to omit this duty and lose out of his home nurture this mighty element of power?

The excuses that are offered for the omission are familiar. One pleads want of time. But he finds time for everything else that he really wants to do. Besides, time taken for duty is never lost. Will not the divine benediction on the day be worth more than the few moments of time it takes to invoke it? Then is there nothing worth living for in this world but business and money-making? Is the culture of

[1] Deut. vi. 6-9.

one's home such a trivial matter that it must be neglected to get a few moments more each day for toiling and moiling in the fields of Mammon? Is the spiritual nurture of one's children so unimportant that it may with impunity be crowded out altogether to give one time to sleep a little later, or read the morning paper more leisurely, or chat with one's neighbors a few minutes longer? But honesty will compel men to confess that this excuse is never offered in sincerity.

Another pleads timidity. He cannot make a prayer in his family. He would break down. But is timidity a sufficient plea to excuse one from a duty so solemn, on which such vital interests of time and eternity depend? We had better test all our actions as we go on through life by inquiring how they will look at the judgment day or from amid their own consequences at the end. When a parent stands at God's bar and this sin of omission is charged against him, will his answer, "I was too diffident," be sufficient to wipe out the charge? If his children, left unblessed in their tender years by the influence of household worship, grow up worldly and godless, drift away in sin and are lost, will it console the father and satisfy him, as he sits in the shadows of his old age and sees their ruin, to say, "I was too timid"?

A Christian mother says that her husband is not a Christian, and that she has never had the courage to establish family worship. But many godly mothers have done so. There are mothers who every morning and every evening gather their children together, sing a hymn with them, read a chapter from God's Word and then bow in prayer invoking heaven's grace upon their heads and upon the beloved father. It would be easy to cite examples proving the power of such hallowed faithfulness. It may at first be a cross for a mother to take up, but, like all crosses taken up for Christ's sake and for love's sake, the burden becomes a joy and an uplifting influence, and out of the hard duty comes such blessing that the hardness is soon forgotten. There are men in heaven to-day or engaged now in earnest Christian service on the earth because their godly wives had the courage to establish a family altar in the home. There are children all over the Christian world in whose hearts the sweetest memory of early years is that of the tender moments in the old home when they bowed in the daily prayer and the mother with trembling tones implored God's blessing upon her household.

It would be easy to add many other words to enforce and illustrate the importance of this duty. If these pages are read by parents who have no household altar, they are affectionately entreated, for the sake of their children, to set it up at once. It will bind the family more closely together. It will sweeten every joy and lighten every burden. It will brighten every path of toil and care. It will throw about the children a holy protection as they go out amid dangers. It will fill their hearts with the truths and influences of the divine Word. It will weave into the memory of their home golden and silver threads which will remain bright forever. It will keep continually open a way between the home and heaven, setting up a ladder from the hearthstone on earth to the Father's house in glory, on which the angels shall come and go continually in faithful ministry. Blessed is the home which has its family altar whose fires never go out. But sad is the home, though it be filled with splendors and with the tenderness of human love, in which the household never gather for united prayer.

It is very important that the family worship be conducted in such a way as to interest the younger members of the household, and even the little children. It ought to be made the brightest and most pleasant exercise of the day. In some instances it is rendered irksome and wearisome. Long chapters are read, and read in a lifeless and unintelligible manner. The prayer is the same day after day, a series of petitions of the most general kind, reaching out over all classes and conditions of men except the little group that kneels about the altar, and embracing all the great needs and wants of the world save the needs and wants of the family itself that bows together. If singing is part of the worship, the psalm or hymn is not carefully chosen for its appropriateness and fitness to the experiences and hearts of those who are to sing it. In the whole exercise there is nothing to win the attention of the children or to interest them in the holy service. It is taken for granted that because it is a religious act it cannot be made pleasant and attractive, that children ought to sit still and listen attentively even if the service is dull and wearisome; and that it is an evidence of their depravity that they fidget and wriggle on their chairs or carry on their sly mischief while the saintly father with closed eyes is droning over his stereotyped prayer.

But there is no reason in the world why religious exercises should be made dull and irksome. The family worship should be of such a character that it would be anticipated with eagerness, and that its memories would ever be among the most hallowed recollections of the childhood's home. Each portion of the exercise should be enlivened by pleasing variety. Instead of being stately and formal, it should be made simple and familiar. Instead of requiring the children to listen in silence while the father goes through the whole worship alone, a part should be given to each member.

Just in what manner it is best to do this each household must decide for itself. Indeed, no one method is always best, as variety is one of the elements of interest. In some families the Scripture is read by verses in turn, every member reading. In others it is read responsively, the leader taking one verse and all the members together the next; in others the father alone reads. The matter of the selection of passages to read is important. Some heads of families follow the order of the Bible itself, going through it in course, not omitting a chapter or a verse, even stumbling over the long lists of names in the Chronicles. Many, in these later days, read the selection assigned for the day in the Home Readings in the Sunday-school lesson-helps. This is a good method, as it aids in the preparation of the lesson for the week, gathering the whole seven days' reading and study around some one Scripture passage in which the children are for the time particularly interested. An occasional topical lesson is pleasant and helpful. For instance, on Sabbath morning let the reading consist of verses in brief passages from different parts of the Bible, all bearing upon the central topic of the day's lesson. On some day in the spring let all the verses that refer to flowers and plants be culled and read. When the first snow falls let all the passages that relate to snow be gathered from the Bible, with an appropriate word concerning each one. It will add to the interest in these exercises if the topic is announced in advance and each member of the family requested to find as many verses as possible bearing upon it. All Scripture-reading in the family worship will be brightened and its interest for children enhanced by an occasional explanatory remark or by an incident that illustrates the thought.

Singing should form part of the worship whenever possible. Occasionally — for instance, on the Sabbath evenings — it will be found profitable to hold a little family service of song, reading a verse or two of Scripture and then singing a stanza of a psalm or hymn appropriate to the sentiment of the Bible passage.

The prayer in the household worship should be brief, particularly where the children are young. It should be fresh, free from all stereotyped phrases, couched in simple language that all can understand. It should be a prayer for the family at whose altar it is offered, not altogether omitting outside interests, but certainly including the interests of the household itself. It should be tender and personal, frequently taking up the members by name and carrying to the Lord the particular needs of each, remembering any who are sick, or in trouble, or exposed to danger or temptation. Some part in the prayer may also be given to the children. If the children are young they may repeat the entire prayer after the father, phrase by phrase. The Lord's Prayer may be used at the close, all uniting in it. In these ways the whole family will be interested in the worship, and it will become a delightful exercise, full of profit and instruction and rich with influences for good.[1]

But family worship is not enough. There are homes where prayer is never omitted, yet in which there is not the spirit of Christ; and only the spirit of Christ in a household makes a truly Christian

[1] "Family Prayer," by the author of this book, gives a brief prayer for every day of the week for three months (price $1.00).

home. If the altar is in the midst the whole life of the home should be filled with the incense that burns upon it. There are some fields of grass from which in summer days rises a sweet fragrance, although not a flower is anywhere to be seen. But when you part the tall grass and look down among its roots, there, close on the ground, hidden under the showy, waving grass, you see multitudes of small flowers, modest and lowly, yet pouring forth a delicate and delicious aroma, filling all the air. There are homes in which there is nothing remarkable in the way of grandeur or elegance, yet the very atmosphere as you enter is filled with sweetness, like "the smell of a field which the Lord hath blessed." It is the aroma of love, the love of Christ shed abroad in human hearts. Religion is lived there. The daily prayers bring down the spirit of heaven. Christ dwells there, and his blessed influence fills with divine tenderness all the home life.

It was said of one that "she looked like a prayer." If we would make our homes truly Christian homes, our daily lives must be like our daily prayers. If the members of the family wrangle and quarrel, the fact that the father is a minister or an elder, and the mother president of a Dorcas society or secretary of an association to send the gospel to China, does not make the home religious. If a blessing is asked at the table before the meal begins, and if then, instead of cheerful and affectionate conversation, the table-talk is made up of faultfinding with the food, of ill-tempered disputes and acrimonious bickerings, the asking of a blessing scarcely makes the intercourse Christian. If family worship is observed with scrupulous fidelity, and the members rise from their knees to violate the simplest lessons of Christian love and kindness in their fellowship as a household, the fact that there is family worship does not make a Christian home. The prayers must be lived. The Scripture lessons must find their way into the heart and then into the speech and conduct. The songs must sing themselves over and over all day in the household intercourse.

A German artist whose fame is world-wide spent eight arduous years in making a marvelous statue of the Saviour. He firmly believed that he had seen Christ in a vision, and that the form he had chiseled in the marble was the very image of the glorious Person he had seen. Afterwards he grew famous, and was asked to make statues of certain heathen deities. But he refused, saying, "A man who has seen Christ would commit sacrilege if he should employ his art in the carving of a pagan goddess. My art is henceforth a consecrated thing." The lips that have breathed the sacred words of family prayer should never speak bitter, angry or unkind words. A home in which the altar has been set up is thenceforth a consecrated spot. To surrender it to bickerings and strifes is sacrilege. It is holy unto the Lord, and should be a scene only of love and tenderness, of joy and peace.

RELIGION IN THE HOME

It is said that in Greenland when a stranger knocks at the door, he asks, "Is God in this house?" If the answer is "Yes," he enters. So blessings and joys pause at our doors and knock to ask if God is in our dwelling. If he is, they enter; if he is not, they flee away, for they will not enter or tarry in a godless home. A young girl engaged in a wealthy but prayerless household as a domestic servant. After spending one night under the roof, she came to her mistress pale and agitated and told her she could not stay with her any longer. When pressed for her reason she at length replied that she was afraid to live and sleep in a house in which there was no prayer. And there are no heavenly blessings that will enter or abide in a prayerless home. No divine guest is there. No wings of love droop down to cover the dwelling. It is a house without a roof, as it were, for it is written that God will pour out his fury upon the families that call not upon his name. But into the home where God abides heaven's richest blessings come, and come to stay. Angels encamp around it. It is roofed over with the wings of God. Its joys are all sweetened by the divine gladness. Its sorrows are all comforted by the divine sympathy. Its benediction rests upon all who go out from its doors. It is but the vestibule to heaven itself.

There is no inheritance which the richest parent can bequeath to a child that can compare for one moment with the influence and blessing of a truly godly home. It gives to the whole trend of the

life, away into the eternal years, such a direction
and such an impulse that no after-influence, no false
teachings, no terrific temptation, no darkening ca-
lamity, can ever altogether turn it away from its
course. For a time it may be drawn aside by some
mighty power of evil, but if the work in the home
has been true and deep, permeating the whole nature,
the deviation from rectitude will be but temporary.
If parents give money to their children, they may
lose it in some of life's vicissitudes. If they bequeath
to them a home of splendor, they may be driven
out of it. If they pass down to them as a heritage
only an honored name, they may sully it. But if
they fill their hearts with the holy influences and
memories of a happy Christian home, no calamity,
no great sorrow, no power of evil, no earthly loss,
can ever rob them of their sacred possessions. The
home songs will sing themselves out again in the years
of toilsome duty. The home teachings will knit
themselves into a fiber of character, rich in its manly
or womanly beauty, and invulnerable as a coat of
mail. The home prayers will bind the soul with
gold chains fast round the feet of God. Then, as
the years go on and the old home of earth is broken
up, it only moves from behind, as it were, and goes
on before, where it draws the soul toward the better
life.

For there is a home of which this earthly home,
even at its best, is but a type. Into that home God
is gathering the great family. The Christian house-

hold that is broken here or scattered shall be re-united there. A father and his son were shipwrecked at sea. They clung to the rigging for a time, and then the son was washed off. The father supposed he was lost. In the morning the father was rescued in an unconscious state, and after many hours awoke in a fisherman's hut, lying on a soft, warm bed. He turned his face, and there lay his son beside him on the same bed. So one by one our families are swept away in the sea of death. Our homes are emptied and our fondest ties are broken. But one in Christ Jesus we shall awake in the other world to see beside us again our loved ones whom we have lost here, yet who have only gone before us into the eternal home.

XII

UNITING WITH THE CHURCH

TO unite with the Church is to take one's place among the followers of the Master. It is a public act. It is a confession of Christ before men. It is not a profession of superior saintliness; on the other hand, it is a distinct avowal of personal sinfulness and unworthiness. Those who seek admission into the church come as sinners, needing and accepting the mercy of God and depending upon the atonement of Christ for the forgiveness of their sins.

They come confessing Christ. They have heard his call, "Follow me," and have responded. Uniting with the Church is taking a place among the friends of Christ; it is coming out from the world to be on Christ's side. There are but two parties among men. "He that is not with me is against me," said Jesus. The Church consists of those who are with Christ. This suggests one of the reasons why those who love Christ should take their place in the Church. By so doing they declare to all the world where they stand and cast all the influence of their life and example on Christ's side.

Secret discipleship fails at this point. However much we may love Christ, however intimate our fellowship with him may be, however sincere our friendship for him, he misses in us the outspoken loyalty of a true confession which proclaims his name in its every breath. Secret discipleship hides its light and fails to honor Christ before men.

Uniting with the Church is a declaration that one has joined the company of Christ's disciples. Disciples are learners. Young Christians have entered the school of Christ — have only entered it. They do not profess to have attained perfection; they profess only to have begun the Christian life.

Jesus took his first disciples into his school and for three years taught and trained them. He made known to them the great truths of Christianity which he had come to reveal — truths about God, about his kingdom on the earth, about duty. Then he taught them how to live.

In like manner the disciples of Christ who enter his Church now become his pupils. They may be very ignorant, but this is no reason why they should not be admitted to the school of the great Teacher. They should not wait to increase their knowledge before they become his disciples. The very purpose of a school is to take those who are ignorant and teach them.

But one condition of admittance as a pupil is, a desire to learn and a readiness to be taught. Of the first Christians, after the day of Pentecost, it is given as one of the marks of new life in them that they continued steadfastly in the apostles' teaching. They were eager to learn all they could hear about Jesus, and therefore they lost no opportunity of listening to the teaching of the apostles, who had been with Jesus for three years. Young Christians should always be eager to learn. This is one of the objects of Church membership.

In different ways is this instruction given. A Christian home should be a school of Christ. The Christian mother is Christ's first apostle to her children who should learn from her lips the great lessons of life. Home teachings come first when the mind is open and the heart is tender and sensitive to impressions. The Sunday-school is designed to do an important work in teaching the young the truths of Christianity. The pastor is a teacher. He has been trained to be an instructor of others in knowledge of God and in the way of life. He expounds the vital truths of the Scriptures and also interprets them for daily life. The private reading of the Bible is another way of learning the things we need to know to make us wise unto salvation.

But knowledge is not all. Even Bible knowledge is not all, does not alone make one a good Christian. One might know all the great facts and doctrines of the Word of God, might be a profound Bible scholar and a wise theologian, and yet not be an advanced or even a growing Christian. We are to learn to live Christ as well as to know the truths about Christ.

Jesus in his teachings makes a great deal of obedience. We are his friends if we do whatsoever he commands us. We are to learn to be patient, meek, gentle, long-suffering, compassionate. We are to learn to be humble, kindly affectioned, unselfish, truthful, sincere.

Young Christians enter Christ's school to be trained in all the qualities which make up the true Christian life. Jesus is not only the teacher, — his life is the textbook which we are to study. Part of his mission to this world was to show us in himself what a true and complete human life is. He was sinless, and he realized the full beauty of obedience to the divine will. We are to look to his life to learn just how to live, the kind of character we are to seek to have, the meaning of the lessons which his words set for us. We are in the school of Christ to be trained in all Christian life and duty.

The lessons the Bible sets for us we are to learn to live out in common life. Every word of Christ sets a copy for us, as it were, and we are to learn to write it in fair and beautiful lines. For example, it is not enough to learn from the Beatitudes that certain qualities are praised by the great Teacher; we are to get the Beatitudes into our own life as quickly and as perfectly as we can. So of all the teachings of Christ — they are not for knowing merely, as one learns the fine sayings of favorite literary writers; they are for living. They are to become lamps to our feet and lights to our path, and they are to be wrought into the web of our character. The object of the Church in this training of disciples is well expressed in the words of Paul, — "for the perfecting of the saints, unto the work of ministering, unto the building up of the body of Christ: till we all attain unto the unity of the faith, and of the knowledge of the Son of God, unto a fullgrown man, unto the measure of the stature of the fulness of Christ."

This thought of the Church as the school of Christ and of young Christians as entering the school is very suggestive. We are not to expect perfection, but we have a right to expect an increasing knowledge of spiritual things and also spiritual growth in all the qualities which belong to Christian character. We should become more patient, more loving, more unselfish, more helpful, more faithful in all duty, more like Christ.

Uniting with the Church brings its duties. It allies us with Christ and makes us coworkers with him. We are not to think merely of what the Church may do for us, but also of what we may do for the Church. Church loyalty is a mark of true and wholesome Christian life. One need not be a narrow sectarian to be a good Church member; but one will always be the better Christian for being entirely devoted to his own church and enthusiastic in all its life and work. Anything that weakens a man's loyalty to his own particular church hurts his spiritual life and lessens his usefulness as a Christian.

In many ways Church members may serve their

church. They should be interested in all its work of saving souls and promoting the cause of Christ. They should regularly attend its services. They should contribute for its support. They should study its interests and seek in every way to extend its influence. They should keep the Church in their prayers, daily making supplication for it. They should bring to it always the best they have to bring, not of gifts and service only, but also of love and personal helpfulness.

It is a high privilege to be a Church member, and one who has such honor should seek to be worthy of it, as the Church is the body of Christ in this world.

XIII

TRANSFORMED BY BEHOLDING

NO sooner do we begin to behold the fair face that looks out at us from the gospel chapters than a great hope springs up in our hearts. We can become like Jesus. Indeed, if we are God's children, we shall become like him. We are foreordained to be conformed to his image. It matters not how faintly the divine beauty glimmers now in our soiled and imperfect lives: some day we shall be like him. As we struggle here with imperfections and infirmities, with scarcely one trace of Christlikeness yet apparent in our life, we still may say, when we catch glimpses of the glorious loveliness of Christ, "Some day I shall be like that."

But how may we grow into the Christlikeness of Christ? Not merely by our own strugglings and strivings. We know what we want to be; but when we try to lift our own lives up to the beauty we see and admire, we find ourselves weighted down. We cannot make ourselves Christlike by any efforts of our own. Nothing less than a divine power is sufficient to produce this transformation in our human nature.

TRANSFORMED BY BEHOLDING

The Scripture describes the process. Beholding the glory of the Lord, we are changed into the image of the glory — that is, we are to find the likeness of Christ, and are to look upon it and ponder it, gazing intently and lovingly upon it, and as we gaze we are transformed and grow like Christ; something of the glory of his face passes into our dull faces and stays there, shining out in us.

We know well the influence on our own natures of things we look upon familiarly and constantly. A man sits before the photographer's camera, and the image of his face prints itself on the glass in the darkened chamber of the instrument. Something like this process is going on continually in every human soul. But the man is the camera, and the things that pass before him cast their images within him and print their pictures on his soul. Every strong, pure human friend with whom we move in sympathetic association does something toward the transforming of our character into his own image. The familiar scenes and circumstances amid which we live and move are in a very real sense photographed upon our souls. Refinement without us tends to the refining of our spirits. The same is true of all evil influences. Bad companionships degrade those who choose them. Thus even of human lives about us it is true that, beholding them, we are transformed into the same image.

But it is true in a far higher sense of the beholding of Christ. It is not merely a brief glance now and

[201]

then that is here implied, not the turning of the eye toward him for a few hurried moments in the early morning or in the late evening, but a constant, loving and reverent beholding of him through days and years till his image burns itself upon the soul. If we thus train our heart's eyes to look at Christ, we shall be transformed into his image.

"Beholding we are changed." The verb is passive. We do not produce the change. The marble can never carve itself into the lovely figure that floats in the artist's mind: the transformation must be wrought with patience by the sculptor's own hands. We cannot change ourselves into the image of Christ's glory: we are changed. The work is wrought in us by the divine Spirit. We simply look upon the image of the Christ, and its blessed light streams in upon us and prints its own radiant glory upon our hearts. We have nothing to do but to keep our eyes fixed upon the mirrored beauty as the flowers hold up their faces toward the sun, and the transformation is divinely wrought in us. It is not wrought instantaneously. At first there are but dimmest glimmerings of the likeness of Christ. We cannot in a single day learn all the long, hard lessons of patience, meekness, unselfishness, humility, joy and peace. Little by little the change is wrought, and the beauty comes out as we continue to gaze upon Christ. Little by little the glory flows into our lives from the radiant face of the Master, and flows out again through our dull lives, transforming them.

But we actively must choose to look.

TRANSFORMED BY BEHOLDING

Even though but little seems to come from our yearnings and struggles after Christlikeness, God honors the yearning and the striving, and while we sit in the shadows of weariness, disheartened with our failures, he carries on the work within us, and with his own hands produces the divine beauty in our souls. There is a pleasant legend of Michelangelo. He was engaged on a painting, but grew weary and discouraged while his work was yet incomplete, and at length fell asleep. Then while he slept an angel came, and, seizing the brush that had dropped from the tired artist's fingers, finished the picture,

> "Wrought the wondrous work — a love-thought carried
> Into colors fit and fair, completed."

Michelangelo awoke at length, affrighted that he had slept and foregone his task in self-indulgence, but, looking at his canvas, his heart was thrilled with joy and his soul uplifted beyond measure, for he saw that while he had slept his picture had been finished, and that it had been

> "painted fairer
> Far than any picture of his making
> In the past, with tint and touch diviner,
> And a light of God above it breaking."

So it is with all who truly long and strive after the heavenly likeness. Faint and discouraged, they think they are making no progress, no growth toward the divine image, but in the very time of their faintness and disheartenment, "when human hands are weary folded," God's Spirit comes and silently fashions the beauty in their souls. When they awake, they shall see the work finished, and shall be satisfied in Christ's likeness.

There is great comfort in this for many of the Father's weary children who earnestly long to become like the Master, and who struggle without ceasing to attain the divine image, but who seem to themselves never to make any progress. God is watching them, sees their strivings, is not impatient with their failures and in the hours of quiet will send his angel to help them. Perhaps the very hours of their deepest discouragement may be the hours when they are growing the most, for then God works most helpfully in them.

There is still another thought. The Revised Version makes a change in the reading of the words about beholding the glory of the Lord, and puts them in this way: "We all, with unveiled face, reflecting as a mirror the glory of the Lord, are transformed into the same image." According to this rendering we, too, become mirrors. We gaze upon the glory of the Lord, and as we gaze the glory streams upon us, and there is an image of Christ reflected and mirrored in us. Then others, looking upon us, see the image of Christ in our lives.

We look into a little pool of still water at night and see the stars in it, or by day and see the blue sky, the passing clouds and the bright sun high in the heavens. So we look upon Christ in loving, adoring

faith, and the glory shines down into our soul. Then
our neighbors and friends about us look at us, see
our character, watch our conduct, observe our dis-
position and temper and all the play of our life, and
as they behold us they perceive the image of Christ
in us. We are the mirrors, and in us men see the
beauty of the Lord.

A little child was thinking about the unseen Christ
to whom she prayed, and came to her mother with
the question, "Is Jesus like anybody I know?" The
question was not an unreasonable one: it was one to
which the child should have received the answer
"Yes." Every true disciple of Christ ought to be
an answer — in some sense, at least — to the child's
inquiry. Every little one ought to see Christ's beauty
mirrored in its mother's face. Every Sunday-school
teacher's character should reflect some tracings of
the eternal Love on which the pupils may gaze.
Whoever looks upon the life of any Christian should
see in it at once the reflection of the beauty of Christ.

Of course the mirroring never can be perfect.
Muddy pools give only dim reflections of the blue
sky and the bright sun. Too often our lives are like
muddy pools. A broken mirror gives a very imper-
fect reflection of the face that looks into it. Many
times our lives are broken, shattered mirrors and
show only little fragments of the glory they are in-
tended to reflect. If one holds the back of a mirror
toward the sun, there will be in it no reflection of the
orb of day; the mirror's face must be turned toward

the object whose image one wants to catch. If we would have Christ mirrored in our lives, we must turn and hold our faces always Christward. If we continue ever beholding the glory, gazing upon it, we shall be mirrors reflecting him into whose face we gaze. Then those who look upon our lives will see in us a dim image at least, a little picture, of Christ.

XIV

BEING CHRISTIANS ON WEEKDAYS

HOW to carry our religion into all parts of our life is the question which perplexes many of us. It is not hard to be good on the quiet Sabbaths, when all the holy influences of the sanctuary and of the Christian home are about us. It is not hard, in such an atmosphere, to think of God, and to yield ourselves to the impact of the divine Spirit. It is easy then to accept the promises and allow them to twine themselves about our weakness, like a mother's arms about feeble infancy. Most of us have little trouble with doubts and fears or with temptations and trials while sitting in the peaceful retreats into which the Sabbath leads us.

Our trouble is in carrying this sweet, holy, restful life out into the weekday world of toil, anxiety, strife and pain. Ofttimes with Monday morning we lose all the Sabbath calm and resume again the old experience of restless distraction. The restraints of godliness lose their power, and the enthusiasm for holy living, so strong yesterday, dies out in the midst of the world's chilling influences, and we drop back into the old habitudes and creep along again in the old dusty ways.

The Sabbath has lifted us up for a day, but has not power to hold us up in sustained elevation of soul. The duties we saw so clearly and so firmly determined to do while sitting in the sanctuary we do not feel pressing upon us to-day with half the urgency of yesterday. Our high resolves and our excellent intentions have proved only like the morning cloud and the early dew; so our religion becomes a sort of luxury to us — a bright unreal dream only which for one day in seven breaks into the worldliness and the self-seeking of our humdrum lives, giving us a period of elevation, but no permanent uplifting. It is only as when one climbs up out of a valley into the pure air of a mountain top for one hour, and then creeps down again and toils on as before amid the mists and in the deep shadows, but carrying none of the mountain's inspiration or of the mountain's splendor with him back into the valley.

Yet such a life has missed altogether the meaning of the religion of Christ, which is not designed to furnish merely a system of Sabbath oases across the desert of life, with nothing between but sand and glare. Both its precepts and its blessings are for all the days. He who worships God only on Sabbaths, and then ignores him or disobeys him on weekdays, really has no true religion. We are perpetually in danger of bisecting our life, calling one portion of it religious and the other secular. Young people, when they enter the Church, are earnestly urged to Christian duty, and the impression made upon them is that Christian duty means reading the Bible and praying every day, attending upon the public means of grace, taking active part in some of the associations, missionary or charitable, which belong to the Church, and in private and personal ways striving to bring others to Christ.

Now, important as these things are, they are by no means all the religious duties of any young Christian, and it is most fallacious teaching that emphasizes them as though they were all.

Religion recognizes no bisecting into sacred and secular. "Whether therefore ye eat, or drink, or whatsoever ye do, do all to the glory of God." It is just as much a part of Christian duty to do one's weekday work well as it is to pray well. "I must be about my Father's business," said Jesus in the dawn of youth; and what do we find him doing after this recognition of his duty? Not preaching nor teaching, but taking up the common duties of common life and putting all his soul into them. He found the Father's business in his earthly home, in being a dutiful child subject to his parents, in being a diligent pupil in the village school and later in being a conscientious carpenter. He did not find religion too spiritual, too transcendental, for weekdays. His devotion to God did not take him out of his natural human relationships into any realm of mere sentiment: it only made him all the more loyal to the duties of his place in life.

We ought to learn the lesson. Religion is intensely

practical. Only so far as it dominates one's life is it
real. We must get the commandments down from
the Sinaitic glory amid which they were first graven
on stone by the finger of God and give them a place
in the hard, dusty paths of earthly toil and struggle.
We must get them off the tables of stone and have
them written on the walls of our own hearts. We
must bring the Golden Rule down from its bright
setting in the teaching of our Lord and get it wrought
into our daily, actual life.

We say in creed, confession and prayer that we
love God, and he tells us, if we do, to show it by
loving our fellow men, since professed love to God
which is not thus manifested is not love at all. We
talk about our consecration; if there is anything
genuine in consecration, it bends our wills to God's,
it leads us to loyalty that costs, it draws our
lives to lowly ministry. "One secret act of self-
denial," says a thoughtful writer, "one sacrifice of
inclination to duty, is worth all the mere good
thoughts, warm feelings, passionate prayers, in which
idle people indulge themselves."

> "Faith's meanest deed more favor bears
> Where hearts and wills are weighed
> Than brightest transports, choicest prayers,
> Which bloom their hour and fade."

We are too apt to imagine that holiness consists
in mere good feeling toward God. It does not: it
consists in obedience in heart and life to the divine
requirements. To be holy is, first, to be set apart

[210]

for God and devoted to God's service: "The Lord hath set apart him that is godly for himself"; but if we are set apart for God in this sense, it necessarily follows that we must live for God. We belong wholly to him, and any use of our life in any other service is sacrilege, as if one would rob the very altar of its smoking sacrifice to gratify one's common hunger. Our hands are God's, and can fitly be used only in doing his work; our feet are God's, and may be employed only in walking in his ways and running his errands; our lips are God's, and should speak words only that honor him and bless others; our hearts are God's, and must not be profaned by thoughts and affections that are not pure.

Ideal holiness is no vague sentiment: it is intensely practical. It is nothing less than the bringing of every thought and feeling and act into obedience to Christ. We are quite in danger of leaving out the element of obedience in our conception of Christian living. If we do this, our religion loses its strength and grandeur and becomes weak, nerveless and force-less. As one has said, "Let us be careful how we cull from the gospel such portions as are congenial, forge God's signature to the excerpt and apply the fiction as a delusive anodyne to our violated con-sciences. The beauties and graces of the gospel are all flung upon a background of requirements as in-flexible as Sinai and the granite. Christ built even his glory out of obedience."

Now, it is the weekday life, under the stress and

Holiness is intensely practical.

We are God's and should honor Him w/ all our heart, soul, mind, & blood

the strain of temptation, far more than the Sunday
life, beneath the gentle warmth of its favoring con-
ditions, that really puts our religion to the test and
shows what power there is in it. Not how well we
sing and pray nor how devoutly we worship on the
Lord's day, but how well we live, how loyally we obey
the commandments, how faithfully we attend to all
our duties, on the other days, tell what manner of
Christians we really are.

Nor can we be faithful toward God and ignore
our human relationships. "It is impossible," says
one, "for us to live in fellowship with God without
holiness in all the duties of life. These things act
and react on each other. Without a diligent and
faithful obedience to the calls and claims of others
upon us, our religious profession is simply dead.
We cannot go from strife, breaches and angry words
to God. Selfishness, an imperious will, want of
sympathy with the sufferings and sorrows of other
men, neglect of charitable offices, suspicions, hard
censures of those with whom our lot is cast, will
miserably darken our own hearts and hide the face
of God from us."

The one word which defines and describes all rela-
tive duties is the word love. Many people under-
stand religion to include honesty, truthfulness,
justice, purity, but do not think of it as including
just as peremptorily unselfishness, thoughtfulness,
kindness, patience, good temper and courtesy. We
are commanded to put away lying, but in the same

paragraph, and with equal urgency, we are enjoined to let all bitterness, wrath, anger, clamor and evil-speaking be put away, and to be kind one to another, tender-hearted, forgiving one another. The law of love in all its most delicate shades of application to spirit, word, act and manner is the law of all true Christian living.

Thus the religion of the Sabbath, like a precious perfume, must pervade all the days of the week. Its spirit of holiness and reverence must flow down into all the paths of everyday life. Its voices of hope and joy must become inspirations in all our cares and toils. Its exhortations must be the guide of hand and foot and finger in the midst of all trial and temptation. Its words of comfort must be as lamps to burn and shine in sick rooms and in the chambers of sorrow. Its visions of spiritual beauty must be translated into reality in conduct and character. visions → conduct & character

So, in all our life, the Sabbath's lessons must be lived out during the week; the patterns of heavenly things shown in the mount must be wrought into forms of reality and act and disposition and character. The love of God which so warms our hearts as we think of it must flow out in love to men. We must be Christians on Monday as well as on the Sabbath. Our religion must touch every part of our life and transform it all into the beauty of holiness.

SHALL WE WORRY?

WHEN you are inclined to worry — don't do it. That is the first thing. No matter how much reason there seems to be for worrying, still, there is your rule. Do not break it: don't worry. Matters may be greatly tangled, so tangled that you cannot see how they ever can be straightened out; still, don't worry. Troubles may be very real and very sore, and there may not seem a rift in the clouds; nevertheless, don't worry.

You say the rule is too high for human observance — that mortals cannot reach it; or you say there must be some exceptions to it — that there are peculiar circumstances in which one cannot but worry. But wait a moment. What did the Master teach? "I say unto you, be not anxious for your life. . . . Be not anxious for the morrow." He left no exceptions. What did Paul teach? "In nothing be anxious." He said not a word about exceptions to the rule, but left it unqualified and absolute. A good bit of homely, practical, common-sense wisdom says that there are two classes of things we should not worry about — things we can help, and things we cannot help. Evils we can help we ought to help. If the roof leaks, we ought to mend it; if the fire is burning low and the room growing cold, we ought to put on more fuel; if the fence is tumbling down, so as to let our neighbor's cattle into our wheat field, we had better repair the fence than sit down and worry over the troublesomeness of people's cows; if we have dyspepsia and it makes us feel badly, we had better look to our diet and our exercise. That is, we are very silly if we worry about things we can help. Help them. That is the heavenly wisdom for that sort of ills or cares: that is the way to cast that kind of burden on the Lord.

But there are things we cannot help. "Which of you by being anxious can add one cubit unto his stature?" What folly, then, for a short man to worry because he is not tall, or for a woman to worry about the color of her hair, or for anyone to worry because of any physical peculiarities he may have? These are types of a large number of things in people's lives which no human power can change. Why worry about these? Will worrying do any good? So we come to the same result by applying this common-sense rule. Things we can make better we should make better, and not fret about them; and things we cannot help or change we should accept as God's will for us, and make no complaint about them. This very simple principle, faithfully applied, would eliminate all worrying from our lives.

[215]

As children of our heavenly Father we may go a step farther. If this world were governed by chance, no amount either of philosophy or of common sense could keep us from worrying; but we know that our Father is taking care of us. No little child in truest and most sheltered home was ever carried so closely or so safely in the love and thought and care of earthly parents as is the least of God's little ones in the heavenly Father's heart. The things we cannot help or change are in his hand, and belong to the "all things" which, we are assured, "work together for good to them that love God." In the midst of all the great rush of events and circumstances in which we can see no order and no design we well know that each believer in Christ is as safe as any little child in the arms of the most loving mother. It is not a mere blind faith that we try to nourish in our hearts as we seek to school ourselves to quietness and confidence amid all life's trials and disappointments: it is a faith that rests upon the character and the infinite goodness of God — the faith of a little child in a Father whose name is "Love" and whose power extends to every part of his universe. So here we find solid rock upon which to stand, and good reason for our lesson that we should never worry. Our Father is taking care of us.

But if we are never to worry, what shall we do with the things that incline us to anxiety? There are many such things in the life even of the most warmly sheltered. There are disappointments that

leave the hands empty after days and years of hope
and toil; there are resistless thwartings of fondly
cherished plans and purposes; there are bereave-
ments that seem to sweep away every earthly joy;
there are perplexities through which no human wis-
dom can lead the feet; there are experiences in every
life whose natural effect is to perturb the spirit and
produce deep and painful anxiety. If we are never
to worry, what are we to do with these things that
naturally tend to cause us worry?

The answer is easy: we are to put all these dis-
turbing and distracting things into the hands of
God. Of course, if we carry them ourselves, we can-
not help worrying over them. But we are not to
carry them; we cannot if we would. Up to the
measure of our wisdom and our ability we are to
forecast our lives and shape our circumstances.
What people sometimes call trust is only indolence;
we must meet life heroically. But when we have
done our whole simple duty, there both our duty
and our responsibility end. We cannot hold back
the wave that the sea flings upon the beach; we
cannot control the winds and the clouds and the
other forces of nature; we cannot keep away the
frosts that threaten to destroy our summer fruits;
we cannot shut out of our doors the sickness that
brings pain and suffering or the sorrow that leaves
its poignant anguish; we cannot prevent the mis-
fortune that comes through others or through public
calamity. In the presence of all this class of ills we

are utterly powerless; they are irremediable by any wisdom or strength of ours. Why, then, should we endeavor to carry them, only to vex ourselves in vain with them?

Besides, there is no reason why we should even try to carry them. It would be a very foolish little child in a home of plenty and of love that should worry about its food and raiment or about its father's business affairs, and be all the while in a state of anxiety and distress concerning its own safety and comfort. The child has nothing whatever to do with these matters; its father and its mother are attending to them.

Or imagine a great ship on the ocean and the child of the ship's captain on board. The child goes about the vessel anxious concerning every movement and worried lest something may go wrong — lest the engines may fail, or the sails give out, or the sailors not do their duty, or the provisions become exhausted, or the machinery break down. What has the captain's child to do with any of these things? The child's father is looking after them.

We are God's children, living in our Father's world, and we have nothing more to do with the world's affairs than the shipmaster's little child has to do with the management and care of the great vessel in midocean. We have only to stay in our place and attend to our own little personal duties, giving ourselves no shadow of anxiety about anything else. That is what we are to do instead of worrying when we meet things that would naturally perplex us. We are just to lay them in God's hands — where they 'belong — that he may look after them while we abide in quiet peace and go on with our little daily duties.

We have high scriptural authority for this. This is what Paul teaches in his immortal prison letter when he says: "Be careful [or anxious] for nothing; but in everything by prayer and supplication, with thanksgiving, let your requests be made known unto God. And the peace of God, which passeth all understanding, shall keep your hearts and your minds through Christ Jesus." The points here shine out very clearly. We are to be anxious in nothing, in no possible circumstances — are never to worry. Instead of being anxious, we are to take everything to God in prayer. The result will be peace: "The peace of God shall keep your hearts and your minds through Christ Jesus." Peter's counsel is similar, though more condensed. In the Revised Version its meaning comes out more clearly: "Casting all your anxiety upon him, because he careth for you." God is taking care of you, not overlooking the smallest thing, and you have but to cast all your anxiety upon him and then be at peace. It is trying to carry our own cares that produces worry; our duty is to cast them all upon Christ, giving ourselves thought only about our duty. This is the secret of peace.

There is a practical suggestion which may be helpful in learning this lesson. The heart in its pressure of care or pain cannot well remain silent; it must speak or break. Its natural impulse is to give utterance to its emotion in cries of pain or in fretful complainings and discontented murmurings. It will be a great relief to the overburdened spirit if in time of pain or trial the pent-up feelings can be given some other vent than in expressions of worry or anxiety. It is most suggestive, therefore, that in Paul's words, already quoted, when he says we should take our anxieties to God in prayer, he adds "with thanksgiving." The songs of thanksgiving carry off the heart's suppressed pain and give it relief.

In "The Marble Faun," Hawthorne makes Miriam, the broken-hearted singer, in the midnight song that went up from the Roman Colosseum, put into the melody the pent-up shriek to which her anguish had almost given vent a moment before: "That volume of melodious voice was one of the tokens of a great trouble. The thunderous anthem gave her an opportunity to relieve her heart by a great cry." It is better always to put pain or grief into melody than into wails. It is better for the heart itself; it is a sweeter relief. There are no wings like the wings of song and praise to bear away life's burdens. Then it is better for the world to start a song trembling in its air than to set loose a shriek or a cry of anguish to fly abroad.

We remember that our Lord, when he was nailed on the cross, where his sufferings must have been excruciating, instead of a cry of anguish turned the woe of his heart into a prayer of intercession for his murderers. Paul, too, in his prison, his back torn with the scourge and his feet fast in the stocks, uttered no word of complaint and no cry of pain, but gave vent to his great suffering in midnight hymns of praise which rang through all the prison.

These illustrations suggest a wonderful secret of heart-peace in the time of distress, from whatever cause. We must find some outflow for our pent-up emotions; silence is unendurable. We may not complain nor give utterance to feelings of anxiety, but we may turn the bursting tides into the channels of praise and prayer.

Then, we may also find relief in loving service for others. Indeed, there is no more wonderful secret of joyful endurance of trial than this. If the heart can put its pain or its fear into helping and comforting those who are in need and in trouble, it soon forgets its own care. If the whole inner story of lives were known, it would be found that many of those who have done the most to comfort the world's sorrow and bind up its wounds and help it in its need have been men and women whose own hearts found outlet for their pain, care or sorrow in ministries to others in Christ's name. Thus they found blessing for themselves in the peace that ruled in their lives, and they became blessings to the world by giving it songs instead of tears, and helpful service instead of the burden of discontent and complaining.

If a bird has to be in a cage, it is better to be a canary to fill its place of imprisonment with happy song than to be a starling to sit dumb within the wire walls in inconsolable distress. If we must have cares and trials, it is better that we should be rejoicing Christians, brightening the very darkness of our environment with the bright light of Christian faith, than that we should succumb to our troubles and get nothing but worry out of our life, and give nothing to the world but murmurings and the memory of our miserable discontent.

LIVING VICTORIOUSLY

LIFE is conflict. Every good thing lies beyond a battlefield, and we must fight our way to it. There must be struggle to get it. This is true in physical life; from infancy to old age existence is a fight with infirmity and disease. In mental life the same is true. Education is a long conflict; the powers of the mind have to fight their way to strength and development. So it is in spiritual life; enemies throng the path and contest every step of progress. No one ever attains to beauty and nobleness of character save through long and sore struggle.

Many of earth's great historic battlefields are now spots of quiet peace. Once men met there in deadly strife — arms clashed, cannon thundered, the air was filled with the shouts of contending armies and the groans of the wounded and dying, and the ground was covered with the dead — but now, in summer days, the grass waves on the once bloody field, sweet flowers bloom, harvests yellow to ripeness, children play and the air is full of bird-songs and the voices of peace. But he who walks over the spot is continually reminded of the terrible struggle which occurred there in the bygone days.

We look upon men and women who have attained high culture of mind and spirit. They are intelligent and educated; they are well balanced in their faculties and symmetrical in their development; their character is strong and noble, showing all the features which belong to true manhood or true womanhood; they are dignified in their deportment, calm and equable in their bearing; they are not hasty in speech nor impetuous in temper; their judgments are never rash; they possess the qualities of patience, contentment and gentleness, combined with courage, righteousness and strength. When we look upon such people, we cannot but admire them and be fascinated by the culture and the majesty and serenity of their lives. We are apt to think of them as highly favored in their original endowment and in their circumstances and experiences.

But if we knew the story of these lives, we should see that where now we behold such ripe and beautiful character was once a battlefield. These men and women began just as all of us must begin — with their faculties undeveloped, their powers undisciplined and their lives uncultured. They had their hard battles with evil in themselves and with evil about them; they grew into intelligence through long and severe mental training and years of diligent study; they attained their splendid self-control through painful experiences of conflict with their tongues, their tempers, their original impetuosity, their many innate propensities to evil; their beauty of Christian character they reached through the submission of their own wills to the will of Christ and of their selfishness and natural resentment and other evil affections and passions to the sway of the spirit of divine love. They were not always what now they are. This noble beauty which we so admire is the fruit of long years of sore struggle, the harvest which has been brought to ripeness by the frosts of autumn, the snows and storms of winter and the rains and sunshine of spring. Back of the calmness, the refinement, the strength and the charming culture which we see is a story of conflict, with many a defeat and many a wounding, and of stern self-discipline, with pain, toil and tears.

We all admire the character of John as it is drawn for us in the New Testament. It seems almost perfect in its affectionateness, its gentleness, its peacefulness. Yet John was not always the saintly man of the Gospel. There is no doubt that he attained this beauty of character, under the transforming influence of Christ's love, through just such sore conflict and self-discipline as all of us must endure to attain Christlikeness. A writer compares the character of this man of love to an extinct volcano he had visited. Where once the crater yawned there is now a verdurous cuplike hollow on the mountain summit; where once the fierce fires had burned lies now a still, clear pool of water, looking up like an eye to the beautiful heavens above, its banks covered with sweet flowers. Says Dr. Culross, speaking of the beloved apostle and referring to this old crater now so beautiful: "It is an apt parable of this man. Naturally and originally volcanic, capable of profoundest passion and daring, he is new-made by grace, till in his old age he stands out in calm grandeur of character and depth and largeness of soul, with all the gentlenesses and graces of Christ adorning him — a man, as I image him to myself, with a face so noble that kings might do him homage, and so sweet that children would run to him for his blessing."

So we learn the story of all noble, cultured character. It is reached only through struggle; it is not natural, but is the fruit of toil and conquest; it bears the marks and scars of many a conflict. We often hear people say they would give large sums to have such a person's contentment, or self-control, or sweetness of disposition, or submissiveness to God's will, or power of giving sympathy. These are things that cannot be bought and that cannot be learned in any school. Such qualities can be gotten only through victorious struggle during years of experience.

We say that Christ gives his disciples this spiritual loveliness, that he renews their natures and transforms their lives, imprinting his own image upon them. This is true; if it were not, there could never be any hope of saintliness in any human life. Yet

Christ does not produce this change in us merely by instantaneously printing his likeness upon our souls as the photographer prints one's picture on the glass in his camera. He works in us, but we must work out the beauty which he puts in germ into our hearts; he helps us in every struggle, yet still we must struggle; he never fights the battle for us, although he is ever near to help us. Thus the noble things of spiritual attainment lie away beyond the hills and the rivers, and we must toil far through strife and pain before we can get them. The old life must be crucified that the new life may emerge. The duty of life is to be victorious. Every good thing, every noble thing, must be won. Heaven is for those who overcome; not to overcome is to fail. In war, to be defeated is to become a slave. To be vanquished in the battle with sin is to become sin's slave; to be overcome by the antagonisms of life is to lose all. But in the Christian life defeat is never a necessity. Over all the ills and enmities of this world we may be victorious.

Moreover, every Christian life ought to be victorious. Jesus said, "In the world ye shall have tribulation: but be of good cheer; I have overcome the world." Nothing will do for a gospel for sinners which leaves any enmity unconquered, any foe unvanquished. Paul, in speaking of the trials and sufferings that beset the Christian — tribulation, distress, persecution, famine, nakedness, sword — asked, "Shall these separate us from the love of

Christ?" That is, "Can these evils and antago-
nisms ever be so great that we cannot overcome
them and be carried still in Christ's bosom?" He
answers his own question by saying triumphantly,
"Nay, in all these things we are more than con-
querors through him that loved us." We need
never be defeated; we may always be victorious.
We may be even "more than conquerors" — tri-
umphant, exultant conquerors. "Whatsoever is born
of God overcometh the world; and this is the victory
that overcometh the world, even our faith."

The ideal Christian life is one, therefore, which
is victorious over all enmity, opposition, difficulty
and suffering. This is the standard which we should
all set for ourselves; this is the pattern shown us
in the holy mount after which we should seek always
to fashion our life. We need never expect to find a
path running along on a level plain, amid sweet
flowers, beneath the shade of the trees.

> "'Does the road wind up hill all the way?' —
> 'Yes, to the end.' —
> 'Will the day's journey take the whole long day?' —
> 'From morn to night, my friend.'"

Of course there will be Elims in the long way,
for God is very loving, but the road will always be
steep and hard. Yet there will never come an ex-
perience in which it will not be wrong for us to be
defeated. Grace has lost none of its power since
New Testament days. Surely the poor stumbling

life so many of us live is not the best possible living for us if we are true Christians. Our Master is able to help us to something far better.

Take temper, the control of the emotion of anger, the government of the tongue. Is there any real reason, any fatal necessity, why we should always be easily provoked, swept away by every slight cause into unseemly passion and into unchristian speech? No doubt Scripture is true to experience when it affirms that the taming of the tongue is harder than the taming of any kind of beast or bird or serpent. No doubt the control of the tongue is the hardest victory to be achieved in all the range of self-discipline, for inspiration affirms that the man who has gotten the complete victory over his speech is a perfectly disciplined man, "able also to bridle the whole body." Yet victory even here is not impossible. The grace of God is sufficient to enable us to live sweetly amid all provocation and irritation, to check all feelings of resentment, to give the soft answer which will turn away wrath and to choke back all rising bitterness before it shall break into a storm of passion. Jesus never lost his temper nor spoke unadvisedly, and he is able to help us to live in the same victorious way.

This is the ideal life for a child of God. We may be more than conquerors. It is not an easy conquest that we may win in a day; in many lives it must be the work of years. Still, it is possible, with Christ to help; and we should never relax our diligence nor withdraw from the battle until we are victorious. He who in the strength of Christ has acquired this power of self-control has reached a sublime rank in spiritual culture. The world may sneer at the man who bears injury and wrong without resentment, without anger, but in God's eyes he is a spiritual hero.

Take trial of any kind — pain, misfortune, sorrow. Is it possible to live victoriously at this point of human experience? Many fail to do so; they succumb to every trial and are overwhelmed by every wave of grief or loss. Many do not make any effort to resist; the faith of their creed, of their hymns, of their prayers, forsakes them, and they meet their troubles apparently as unsupported and unsustained as if they were not Christians at all. A novelist describes one in grief as he stands on the shore and gazes at the ship that is bearing away from him the object of his heart's devotion. In his absorbing anguish he does not observe that the tide is rising. It rolls over his feet, but he is unconscious of it. Higher and higher the waters rise — now to his knees, now to his loins, now to his breast. But all his thought is on the receding ship, and he is oblivious to the swelling of the waves, and at length they flow over his head and he is swept down to death. This is a picture of many of earth's sufferers in sorrow or in misfortune. They are defeated and overborne; the divine promises do not sustain them, because they lose all faith; they hear the words, "Ye sorrow not, even as others which have no hope," and yet they do sorrow just as if they had no hope.

But this is not the best that our religion can do for us. It is designed to give us complete victory in all trial. "As sorrowing yet always rejoicing" is the scriptural ideal for a Christian life. Christ has bequeathed his own peace to his believing ones. We know what his peace was; it was never broken for a moment, though his sorrows and sufferings surpassed in bitterness anything this earth has ever known in any other sufferer. The same peace he offers to each one of his people in all trial.

The artist painted life as a sea, wild, swept by storms, covered with wrecks. In the midst of this troubled scene he painted a great rock rising out of the waves, and in the rock, above the reach of the billows, a cleft with herbage growing and flowers blooming, and in the midst of the herbage and the flowers a dove sitting quietly on her nest. It is a picture of the Christian's heritage of peace in tribulation. It is thus Christ would have us live in the world — in the midst of the sorest trials and adversities always victorious, always at peace. The secret of this victoriousness is faith — faith in the unchanging love of God, faith in the unfailing grace and help of Christ, faith in the immutable divine promises. If we but believe God and go forward ever resolute and unfaltering in duty, we shall always be more than conquerors.

XVII

SHUT IN

THERE are many people who belong to the "shut-ins." They are found in fine city mansions and in quiet country homes, in the dwellings of the rich and in the cottages of the poor. They are invalids who because of their broken health cannot any longer run the race with the swift or fight the battle with the strong; they have been wounded in the strife and have fallen out of the ranks. Passers-by on the street sometimes see their faces at the window, white and bearing marks of suffering, but they no longer mingle with the hurrying throngs nor take their places with the busy toilers. They are "shut in."

They represent many degrees of invalidism. Some of them are almost entirely helpless. Here is one who for many years has not lifted a hand nor moved a finger by her own volition; here is one only partially powerless, unable to walk, but having the use of hands and arms; another has not sufficient strength for any active out-door duty, but can move about the house and perform many a sweet ministry of love. Thus these "shut-ins" embrace all degrees of suffering

and of helplessness, but they are alike in their inability
to join the ranks of the busy workers without. They
must stay in-doors; in a sense, they are prisoners
in this great bright world, no longer free to go where
they would or to do what they earnestly crave to do.

This book may find its way into the hands of some
of these "shut-ins," and it ought to have its message
for them. The message ought also to be one of
cheer and gladness. I would like to write for such
"prisoners of the Lord" a word that may carry com-
fort and strength, that may be to them like a little
flower sent in from the outside, a token of sympathy
laden also with fragrance from the garden of the Lord.

In the account of the entering of Noah into the
ark, before the Flood came, we read that "the Lord
shut him in." For quite a year Noah and his family
were "shut-ins," but it must have been a comfort
for them to know that the shutting of the door was
not accidental — that the Lord had done it. There
was another comfort: it was very much better inside
than outside. Without, there were great storms,
wild torrents and terrible destruction. No man
could live in the rushing waters. Within, there was
perfect safety. Not a drop of rain dashed in; no
wild tempest swept through the door. The ark was a
chamber of peace floating quietly and securely in the
midst of the most terrible ruin the world ever saw.
The Lord's shutting in of his people was to save them.

May we not say of every shut-in child of God,
"The Lord shut him in"? What the Lord does

for his own people can never be unkindness, what-
ever it may seem to be. It is an infinite comfort,
therefore, to a Christian who is kept within doors by
invalidism or other like cause to be able to say, "It
was the Lord who shut me in."

May we not go a step farther and say of such
"shut-ins" that the Lord has shut them in because
it is better for them to be within than without?
No doubt there is protection in such a condition.
These prisoners of the Lord are not exposed to the
storms; it is always warm and safe where they are.
They are dwelling under the shadow of God's wing.
They miss many of the struggles with temptation
and many of the sterner conflicts of life by being
shut in. The ark was guided by an unseen Hand
over the trackless waters of the Deluge. It had no
rudder, no pilot, no sail, no chart, yet it struck no
rock, was whelmed in no wild billows, moved in
no wrong course, and bore its "shut-ins" in safety to
the shores of a new world. May we not say that in
like manner all the "shut-ins" of God's people are
God's peculiar care? Are they not of those whom
he gathers in his arms and carries in his bosom?
We are told that the Lord knoweth how to deliver
the godly out of temptation; may we not say that one
of the ways he delivers from temptation is by shutting
his people away from the rough blasts? No doubt
many a soul has been saved from the evil influences
of worldliness by being called from the midst of the
excitements and strifes of active life into the quiet

shelter of invalidism. The chamber of suffering proves a sanctuary rather than a prison.

But there are other comforts. It is a great deal better to be shut in than to be shut out. There are pictures of both classes in the New Testament. In one of the parables of our Lord the door was shut, and it excluded some who came too late to be admitted; but the same door also shut in with Christ those who had entered in time. No condition could be more suggestive of blessedness than to be shut in with the Master. The closed doors are pledge that there can be no interruption of the communion. Christ's "shut-ins" have abundant opportunity for loving fellowship with him. Their sick rooms are not prisons, but Bethels where Christ comes to meet with them and to bless them.

It is not strange, therefore, that many of the quiet rooms where Christ's disciples are shut in are places of great joy. Faith triumphs over pain. The darkness brings out the stars of promise, and they shine in radiant beauty. Because of infirmity the power of Christ rests in especial measure upon his suffering ones, and they are enabled to rejoice in their very tribulations. Their joy is rich and deep. It is not the rippling surface-happiness of those outside who have no pain and are free to go where they will and to do as they desire: it is heart-joy which does not depend upon external things, and is therefore unaffected by external experiences. There are fresh-water springs that bubble up beneath the edge of the sea; the brackish tides roll over them, but they remain ever sweet and fresh. Like these springs are the fountains of Christian joy. Under the billows of trial and suffering they flow on unwasting and unembittered. Many Christian invalids become almost marvels of patience and peace as they are brought into living communion with Christ. They are never heard complaining; they believe in the love of God, submit themselves to his will and take pain from his hand as confidently and sweetly as they take medicine from their trusted physicians; their faces shine with the radiance of indwelling peace, and the joy of their hearts finds expression in words and songs of praise. Surely, to the angels, as they look down from their pure glory, the chambers in which many of Christ's "shut-ins" lie must appear as spots of bright beauty in this dark world.

We naturally suppose that when persons are laid aside by illness and shut away in quiet sick rooms their work ceases and their usefulness is at an end. After that they are a burden to others instead of being helpers. So we would say. They require tending, watching, nursing; probably they have to be lifted by their friends and carried from chair to bed, from room to room, up and down stairs; they can no longer take any part in the duty of the household nor perform any active service for the Master. We would say at first thought that they are no longer useful; their old-time work has dropped from their hands, and others now have to do it. Yet we greatly mistake when we suppose they are no longer of any service: they have a ministry even in their suffering which in many cases exceeds in value their highest usefulness in their most active days. It is impossible to measure the influence in a home, day after day, of a patient, rejoicing Christian sufferer. There pours out from the sick room of such a "shut-in" a spiritual warmth of love which diffuses itself through all the household life like a summer atmosphere, leaving benediction everywhere.

It was my privilege to visit very often a Christian young woman who for years was a sufferer. Much of the time her pain was excruciating — almost unendurable; but as I watched her from week to week I saw continually the putting forth of new spiritual beauties in her character. Her young life seemed to me like a lovely rosebush in early summer with its many opening buds, and pain was as the summer warmth that caused the buds to burst into full, rich beauty and fragrance. Every time I saw her some new feature of Christlikeness appeared in her life: another rose had opened into full bloom. In her last months there was no opportunity for active service, yet I believe the good she wrought by her ministry of pain far surpassed that which she could have done in the same time with the busiest hands had she lived in painless health. By her suffering she touched the hearts of parents and friends and drew out their sympathy as they watched month after month beside her. These fruits of her pain

will remain as permanent enrichment of the characters
of those who loved her. Another effect of her suffer-
ing was in the influence of her sweet patience. She
never murmured; her faith was never clouded for an
instant; she was gentle, thoughtful, joyous, even in
the sorest pain. Thus she was preaching perpetually
sermons without words on the power of the love and
grace of God, and thus became a blessing to every-
one who entered her room and looked upon her
radiant face.

From very humble life there comes this pathetic
incident which illustrates the same truth: In a pottery
there was a workman who had one small invalid child
at home. The man wrought at his trade with ex-
emplary fidelity. He managed, however, to bear
each evening to the bedside of his "wee lad" a flower,
a bit of ribbon or a fragment of crimson glass — any-
thing that would lie on the white counterpane and
give color to the room. He never went home at
night without something that would make the wan
face light up with joy at his return. He never said
that he loved his boy, and yet he went on patiently
loving him until the whole shop had been drawn into
real though unconscious fellowship with him. The
workmen made curious little jars and cups, and
painted diminutive pictures on them, and burnt them
in their kilns. One brought some fruit and another
some engravings in a scrapbook. Not one of them
whispered a word, for this solemn thing was not to
be talked about. They put their little gifts in the

old man's hat, and he found them there and understood it all. The entire pottery-full of men of rather coarse fiber by nature grew quiet as the months passed, becoming gentle and kind; some dropped swearing as the weary look on their patient fellow worker's face told them beyond mistake that the inevitable shadow was drawing nearer.

Every day some one did a piece of work for him, so that he could come later and go earlier. And when the bell tolled and the little coffin came out of the lonely door, there stood a hundred stalwart workingmen from the pottery with their clean clothes on, losing their half-day's time from work for the privilege of following to the grave that little child whom probably not one of them had ever seen.

These incidents illustrate the refining, softening influence that went out from even a child's sick room and touched a hundred men. All over the country there are other chambers of suffering from which there goes out continually a power that makes men and women quieter, gentler, more thoughtful and kind. Thus God's "shut-ins" are means of grace ofttimes to whole communities.

It is known to many that there is a most helpful system of communication established among invalids over this country with these objects: 1. To relieve the weariness of the sick room by sending and receiving letters and other tokens of remembrance; 2. To testify of the love and presence of Christ in suffering and privation; 3. To pray for one another at set times — daily at twilight hour and weekly on Tuesday morning at ten o'clock; 4. To stimulate faith, hope, patience and courage in fellow sufferers by the study and presentation of Bible promises.

This simple exchanging of consolation among hundreds and thousands of "shut-ins" throughout the country is in itself a ministry whose helpfulness never can be estimated. Whatever tender comfort one finds is passed to others that they may share it. Strong friendships are formed between those who have never met. The hearts of all the great scattered company are drawn into loving sympathy as they think of and pray for one another.

Those who are happy and strong, rejoicing in health and in physical freedom, should never forget these "shut-ins." There are one or more of them in every community. There are many ways in which strength and comfort may be sent to them. A kindly letter now and then, full of cheer and affection, may be like an angel's visit to a weary sufferer. Or the thoughtfulness may be shown by sending a book or some flowers or a little basket of fruit or other token of love. In some cases personal visits are also practicable. There is some way, at least, in which everyone may do a little to lighten the burden of invalidism in some weary sufferer; and surely of all such Jesus will say, "Ye did it unto me."

XVIII

COMING TO THE END

LIFE is a kaleidoscope; every moment the view changes. The beautiful things of one glance are missing at the next, while new things — just as lovely, though not the same — appear in their place. The joys we had yesterday we do not have to-day, though our hearts may be quite as happy now, with gladness just as pure and deep. In a sense, to most of us, life is routine, an endless repetition — the same tasks, the same duties, the same cares, day after day, year after year; yet even in this routine there is constant change. There is an interstitial life that flows through the channel of our daily experiences and that is ever new. We meet new people, we have new things, we read new books, we see new pictures, we learn new facts, while at the same time many of the familiar things are continually dropping out of our lives. The face we saw yesterday we miss to-day, and there are new faces in the throng; the songs we sang last year we do not sing this year; the books we used to read with zest we do not care for any longer; the pleasures that once delighted us have no more charm for us; the toys that meant so much to childhood and were so real have no fascination whatever for manhood and for womanhood; the happy days of youth, with their sports and games, their schools and studies, their friendships and visions, are left behind, though never forgotten, as we pass on into actual life with its harder tasks, its rougher paths, its heavier burdens, its deeper studies, its sterner realities. So we are ever coming to the end of old things and to the beginning of new things. We keep nothing long.

This is true of our friendships. Our hearts are made to love and to cling. Very early the little child begins to tie itself to other lives by the subtle cords of affection. All through life we go on gathering friends and binding them to us by ties of varying strength, sometimes slight as a gossamer thread and as easily broken, sometimes strong as life itself — the very knitting of soul to soul. Yet our friendships are ever changing. Some of them we outgrow and leave behind us as we pass from childhood and youth to maturity; some of them have only an external attachment, and easily fall off and are scarcely missed and leave no scar. This is true of many of our associations in business, in society, in life's ordinary comminglings. We are thrown into more or less intimate relations with people, not by any attractive affinity, any drawing of heart, but by circumstances; and, while there may be pleasant congeniality, there is no real blending or weaving together, life with life; consequently, the ending of such associations produces no sore wrench or pain, no heart-pang. All through life these friends of circumstances are changing; we have the same no two successive years.

In every true life there is an inner circle of loved ones who are bound to us by ties woven out of our very heart's fibers. The closest of these are the members of our own household. The child's first friend is the child's mother; then comes the father; and then the other members of the family are taken into the sacred clasp of the opening life. By and by the young heart reaches outside and chooses other friends from the great world of common people and out of the multitude of passing associates, and binds them to itself with friendship's strongest cords. Thus all true men and true women come up to mature years clustered about by a circle of friends who are dear to them as their own life. Our debt to our life's pure and holy friendships is incalculable; they make us what we are. The mother's heart is the child's first schoolroom. The early home-influences give their tints and hues to the whole after-life; a gentle home where only kindly words are spoken and loving thoughts and dispositions are cherished fills with tender beauty the lives that go out from its shelter. All early friendships print their own stamp on the ripening character. Our souls are like the sensitive plates which the photographer puts into his camera, which catch every image whose reflection falls upon them and hold it ready to be brought out in the finished picture. Says George Macdonald:

THE HOME BEAUTIFUL

> I think that nothing made is lost —
>   That not a moon has ever shone,
> That not a cloud my eyes hath crossed,
>   But to my soul is gone;
>
> · That all the lost years garnered lie
>   In this thy casket, my dim soul,
> And thou wilt, once, the key apply
>   And show the shining whole.

True in general, this is especially true of the pure friendships of our lives. None of the impressions that they make on our lives are ever lost; they sink away into our souls, and then reappear at length in our character.

But even these tender and holy friendships we cannot keep forever; one by one they fall off or are torn out of our lives. There are many ways of losing friends. Sometimes, without explanation, without offense or a shadow of a reason of which we know, without hint or warning given, our friend suddenly withdraws from us and goes his own way, and through life we never have hint or token of the old friendship.

> "Oh, what was the hour and the day,
>   The moment, I lost you?
> I thought you were walking my way;
>   I turned to accost you,
>
> "And silence and emptiness met
>   My word half unspoken.
>   .   .   .   .   .   .
>
> "Oh, what was the hour and the day,
>   The moment, you left me,
> When you went on your separate way,
>   Oh, friend, and bereft me?"

Some friends are lost to us, not by any sudden rupture, but by a slow and gradual falling apart which goes on imperceptibly through long periods, tie after tie unclasping until all are loosed, when hearts once knit together in holy union find themselves hopelessly estranged. A little bird dropped a seed on a rock. The seed fell into a crevice and grew, and at length the great rock was rent asunder by the root of the tree that sprang up. So little seeds of alienation sometimes fall between two friends, and in the end produce a separation which rends their friendship and sunders them forever.

> "No sudden treason turns
> The long-accustomed loyalty to hate,
> But years bring weariness for sweet content;
> And fondness, daily sustenance of love,
> Which use should make a tribute easier paid,
> First grudged, and then withheld, the heart is starved;
> And, though compassion or remorseful thought
> Of happy days departed bring again
> The ancient tenderness in seeming flood,
> Not less it ebbs and ebbs till all is bare."

No picture could be sadder than this, but the saddest thing about it is its truthfulness and the frequency of its repetition in actual life. Many a friendship is lost by this slow process of imperceptibly growing apart.

Then, friends are lost through misunderstandings which in many cases a few honest words at first might have removed. The Scriptures say, "A whisperer separateth chief friends." Friends are lost, too, in the sharp competitions of business, in the keen rivalries of ambition; for love of money or of fame or of power or of social distinction many throw away holy friendships.

Friends are lost, too, by death. Often this process begins early; a child is bereft of father or of mother, or of both. All through life the sad story of bereavement goes on. As the leaves are torn from the trees by the rude storm, so are friendships plucked from our lives by Death's remorseless hand. There is something inexpressibly sad in the loneliness of old people who have survived the loss of nearly all their friends, and who stand almost entirely alone amid the gathering shadows of their life's eventide. Once they were rich in human affection. Children sat about their table and grew up in their happy home; many other true hearts were drawn to them along the years. But one by one their children are gathered home into God's bosom, until all are gone. Other friends — some in one way and some in another — are also removed. At last husband or wife is called away, and one only survives of the once happy pair, lonely and desolate amid the ruin of all earthly gladness and the tender memories of lost joys.

Were it not for the Christian's hope, these losses of friends along the years would be infinitely sad, without alleviation. But the wonderful grace of God comes not only with its revelation of after-life, but with its present healing. God binds up his people's hearts in their sorrow and comforts them in their loneliness. The children and the friends

COMING TO THE END

who are gone are not lost; hand will clasp hand again and heart will clasp heart in inseparable reunion. The grave is only winter, and after winter comes spring with its wonderful resurrections, in which everything beautiful that seemed lost comes again.

We come to the end, also, of many of our life's visions and hopes as the years go on. Flowers are not the only things that fade; morning clouds are not the only things that pass away; sunset splendors are not the only gorgeous pictures that vanish. What comes of all childhood's fancies, of youth's daydreams and of manhood's and womanhood's vision-fabrics? How many of them are ever realized? Life is full of illusions. Many of our ships that we send out to imagined lands of wealth to bring back to us rich cargoes never return at all, or, if they do, only creep back empty with torn sails and battered hulks. Disappointments come to all of us along life's course. Many of our ventures on life's sea are wrecked and never come back to port; many of our ardent hopes prove only brilliant bubbles that burst as we grasp them.

Yet if we are living for the higher things — the things that are unseen and eternal — the shattering of our life's dreams and the failures of our earthly hopes are only apparent losses. The things we can see are but the shadows of things we cannot see. We chase the shadow, supposing it to be a reality; it eludes us and we do not grasp it, but instead we clasp in our hand that invisible thing of which the

visible was only the shadow. A young man has his visions of possible achievement and attainment; one by one, with toil and pain, yet with quenchless ardor, he follows them. All along his life to its close bright hopes shine before him, and he continues to press after them with unwearying quest. Perhaps he does not realize one of them, and he comes to old age with empty hands — an unsuccessful man, the world says — yet all the while his faith in God has not faltered, and he has been gathering into his soul the treasures of spiritual conquest; in his inner life he has been growing richer every day. The struggle after earthly possession may have yielded nothing tangible, but the struggle has developed strength, courage, faith and other noble qualities in the man himself. The bright visions faded as he grasped them, leaving nothing but disappointment; yet if his quest was worthy, he is richer in spirit.

Thus, God gives us friends, and our heart's tendrils twine about them; they stay with us for a time, and then leave us. Our loss is very sore, and we go out bereft and lonely along life's paths. Even love seems to have been in vain, yielding nothing in the end but sorrow. It seems to us that we are poorer than if we had never loved at all; we have nothing left of all that was so precious to us. But we have not lost all. Loving our friends drew out to ripeness the possibilities of love in our own hearts; then the friends were taken away, but the ripened love remains. Our hearts are empty, but our lives are larger. So it is with

all our experiences of disappointment and loss if our hearts are fixed on Christ and if we are living for the invisible things; we miss the shadow only to clasp in heart-possession the imperishable reality. The illusions of faith and hope and love are but the falling away of the rude scaffolding used in erecting the building, that the beautiful temple itself may stand out in enduring splendor.

We come also to the end of trials and sorrows. Every night has a morning, and, however dark it may be, we have only to wait a little while for the sun to rise, when light will chase away the gloom. Every black cloud that gathers in the sky and blots out the blue or hides the stars passes away ere long; and when it is gone there is no stain left on the blue and not a star's beam is quenched or even dimmed. The longest winter that destroys all life and beauty in field, forest and garden is sure to come to an end, giving place to the glad springtime which reclothes the earth in verdure as beautiful as that which perished. So it is with life's pains and troubles. Sickness gives place to health. Grief, however bitter, is comforted by the tender comfort of divine love. Sorrow, even the sorest, passes away and joy comes again, not one glad note hushed, its music even enriched by its experience of sadness.

> "No note of sorrow but shall melt
> In sweetest chord unguessed;
> No labor, all too pressing felt,
> But ends in quiet rest."

THE HOME BEAUTIFUL

Thus in a Christian life no shadow lingers long. Then it will be but a little time till all shadows shall flee away before heaven's glorious light, when forever life will go on without a pain or a sorrow.

There is another ending: we shall come to the end of life itself. We shall come to the close of our last day; we shall do our last piece of work, and take our last walk, and write our last letter, and sing our last song, and speak our last "Good-night"; then to-morrow we shall be gone, and the places that have known us shall know us no more. Whatever other experiences we may have or may miss, we shall not miss dying. Every human path, through whatever scenes it may wander, must bend at last into the Valley of Shadows.

Yet we ought not to think of death as calamity or disaster; if we are Christians, it will be the brightest day of our whole life when we are called to go away from earth to heaven. Work will then be finished, conflict will be over, sorrow will be past, death itself will be left behind, and life in its full, true, rich meaning will only really begin.

The criticalness of life should lead us to be always ready for death. Though we are plainly taught by our Lord not to be anxious about anything that the future may have in store for us, we are as plainly taught to live so as to be prepared for any event which may occur. Indeed, the only way to eliminate care from our present is to be ready for any possible future. Death is not merely a possible, but is an inevitable, event in everyone's future; we can live untroubled by dread of it only by being ever ready for it. Preparation for death is made by living a true Christian life. If we are in Christ by faith, and then follow Christ, doing his will day by day, we are prepared for death, and it can never surprise us unready.

> "It matters little what hour o' the day
> The righteous falls asleep: death cannot come
> To him untimely who is fit to die.
> The less of the cold earth, the more of heaven;
> The briefer life, the longer immortality."

True preparation for death is made when we close each day as if it were the last. We are never sure of to-morrow; we should leave nothing incomplete any night. Each single separate little day should be a miniature life complete in itself, with nothing of duty left over. God gives us life by days, and with each day he gives its own allotment of duty — a portion of his plan to be wrought out, a fragment of his purpose to be accomplished by us. Says F. W. Faber, "Every hour comes with some little fagot of God's will fastened upon its back." Our mission is to find that bit of divine will and do it. Well-lived days make completed years, and the years well lived as they come make a life beautiful and full. In such a life no special preparation of any kind is needed; he who lives thus is always ready. Each day prepares for the next, and the last day prepares for glory. Susan Coolidge writes:

[251]

THE HOME BEAUTIFUL

If I were told that I must die to-morrow —
    That the next sun
Which sinks should bear me past all fear and sorrow
    For anyone,
All the fight fought, all the short journey through —
    What should I do?

I do not think that I should shrink or falter,
    But just go on,
Doing my work, nor change nor seek to alter
    Aught that is gone,
But rise and move and love and smile and pray
    For one more day;

And, lying down at night for a last sleeping,
    Say in that ear
Which hearkens ever, "Lord, within thy keeping
    How should I fear?
And when to-morrow brings thee nearer still,
    Do thou thy will."

If we thus live, coming to the end of life need have no terror for us. Dying does not interrupt life for a moment. Death is not a wall cutting off the path, but a gate through which passing out of this world of shadows and unrealities we shall find ourselves in the immediate presence of the Lord and in the midst of the glories of the eternal home.

We need have only one care — that we live well our one short life as we go on, that we love God and our neighbor, that we believe on Christ and obey his commandments, that we do each duty as it comes to our hand, and do it well. Then no sudden coming of the end will ever surprise us unprepared. Then, while glad to live as long as it may be God's will to leave us here, we shall welcome the gentle angel who comes with the golden joy to lead us to rest and home.

CPSIA information can be obtained
at www.ICGtesting.com
Printed in the USA
BVOW10s0302220717
489695BV00009B/108/P